SPICE POWER

The Inside Story

Rob McGibbon

D0044093

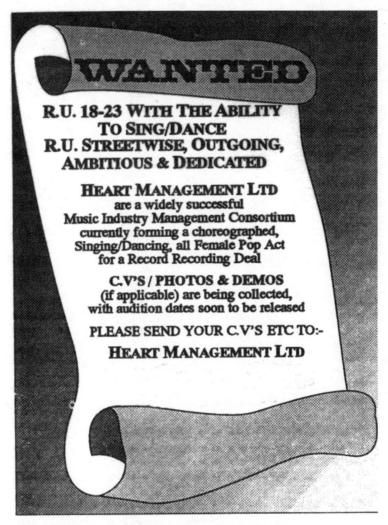

WANTED

R.U. 18-23 WITH THE ABILITY
TO SING/DANCE
R.U. STREETWISE, OUTGOING,
AMBITIOUS & DEDICATED

HEART MANAGEMENT LTD
are a widely successful
Music Industry Management Consortium
currently forming a choreographed,
Singing/Dancing, all Female Pop Act
for a Record Recording Deal

C.V'S / PHOTOS & DEMOS
(if applicable) are being collected,
with audition dates soon to be released

PLEASE SEND YOUR C.V'S ETC TO:-

HEART MANAGEMENT LTD

A white flyer, smaller than the average postcard, displays
a WANTED scroll in the style of a Wild West poster.
It appeals for girls who are 'Streetwise, Outgoing, Ambitious,
Dedicated' to join what is rather weakly described as
a 'Female Pop Act'.

Back in 1993, a thousand or so flyers identical to this were
handed out to selected girls across Britain, and marked the
first step in the creation of the most staggering pop
phenomenon for decades: the Spice Girls.

What follows is the remarkable story of their rise
to pop superstardom.

SPICE POWER

The Inside Story

B⬛XTREE

First published in 1997 by Boxtree, an imprint of Macmillan Publishers Ltd, 25 Eccleston Place, London, SW1W 9NF and Basingstoke

Associated companies throughout the world

Copyright © 1997 Rob McGibbon

ISBN 0 7522 1142 0

9 8 7 6 5 4 3

A CIP catalogue record for this book is available from the British Library

Cover by Dan Newman
Typeset and inside design by Blackjacks

Printed and bound in Great Britain by Mackays of Chatham plc, Chatham, Kent

Neither the Spice Girls nor any of their representatives have had any involvement with this book.

Picture Credits
All Action: front cover; inside picture section – pages 1, 2, 3, 4, 5, 6, 7, 8, 9 *bottom*, 11 *bottom*, 12 *top*, 14 *bottom*, 15.
Capital Pictures: back cover; inside picture section – pages 11 *top*, 12 *bottom*, 14 *top*, 16.
Retna: inside picture section – pages 9, 10 *top*, 13.

CONTENTS

ACKNOWLEDGEMENTS

I'm grateful to many people who kindly helped in the research and production of this book. It's not possible to mention everyone by name, but certain people deserve a special thank you.

I would like to thank everyone who generously gave their time for interviews, particularly the Spice Girls' singing teacher, Pepi Lemer; their first songwriter, Erwin Keiles; and Tim Hawes, the man who helped give them their name and Shelley D'Silva, who helped select the girls at the auditions. My thanks also to Ian Lee and the staff at Trinity Studios, who provided so much information on the formative months of the group and everyone else who provided details and vital information. I'm also grateful for the use of articles in various publications, including the *Express* and magazines such as *Sugar* and *Pride*.

Many people at Boxtree have worked hard to bring this book out swiftly and in particular my thanks go to Adrian Sington, Clare Hulton and to my editor Emma Mann. Also, I am very grateful to my agent Jonathan Lloyd for his work and his advice.

On a personal note, I would like to mention my workaholic friend Simon Lee for no other reason than for being a good mate; and, as always, my special thanks to my family for their constant support in everything. Finally, I would like to make a special acknowledgement to my father for the books we wrote together and, more importantly, for being a true pal.

Rob McGibbon, June 1997

–1–

THE SPICE TRAIL

The girls arrived early that morning. Many were milling around in the street long before the Dance Works studios opened as usual at 9.30 am. But they didn't mind waiting because the audition was too important to miss; it was the day the line-up for a new all-girl pop group would be chosen.

It was Friday, 4 March 1994, and London's Oxford Street was already filled with the noisy hubbub of a typical weekday morning. The girls were in Balderton Street, a quiet side road just off the shopping thoroughfare by Selfridges, but they shut out the frantic West End rush to focus on the audition ahead and the dreams it could make come true.

The buzz about the new group had started ten days earlier when a small advert in the entertainment trade newspaper, the *Stage*, had appealed for girls aged eighteen to twenty-three to join a 'female pop act'. There was one big difference between this ad and the usual ones for theatre shows and television castings: it offered an open audition to *all* hopefuls, with no restrictions on professional training or height and looks. Yes, they needed to be able to sing and dance, but the principal requirements were for them to be 'Streetwise, Outgoing, Ambitious, Dedicated'. Basically, it was a chance for ordinary girls to have a shot at stardom.

The audition was due to start at 11am and, as the time drew nearer, more than 300 girls mingled around Dance Works, an old converted five-storey house. Nervous chatter and the sounds of sleepy singing voices being woken up with vocal exercises echoed through the building. A queue of girls sitting on the rough green carpet snaked its way up the stairs to the main studio door on the third floor. Some girls seemed relaxed and chatted animatedly while others sat quietly, contemplating what lay ahead; most were stretching their supple bodies in preparation for dancing or were reading through the lyric sheet of the song they would sing.

No matter how they filled those minutes before the start, all of them were trying to control the nerves that were tying gut-wrenching knots in the pits of their stomachs. OK, it was just another audition, but they ached to do well. This could be the day that would turn them into pop stars of the future.

There was one man who was also feeling nervous that day – Chris Herbert. The audition was his idea and he had been worrying if enough girls would turn up, so he felt a deep sense of relief when he saw it was a good turn-out. He only needed five girls, and surely they would be amongst this vast group.

Chris's journey to that audition had begun four months earlier when he had the idea that would mushroom into the biggest music sensation since the Beatles. At that time in 1993 Britain and Europe were in the first stages of Take That mania. The five lads from Manchester, led by Gary Barlow, had just scored two consecutive No. 1 hits with 'Pray' and 'Relight My Fire' and were heading for their third with 'Babe'. It was hailed as a time when pop music came back to Britain.

The minds of major record industry executives started coming up with ideas to cash in on Take That's success and it marked an explosion in boy bands based around the same format. The one that would emerge as the front runner in that cloning process was

Boyzone, who would eventually take over the teen-band crown from Take That. Amazingly, despite all the experience and high salaries in the record industry, it fell to Chris Herbert, a twenty-two-year-old novice from Surrey who had been in the business just two years, to come up with the idea that would eclipse all boy bands.

Chris was a natural entrepreneur with an eye for the main chance. He had studied electrical engineering at college, but had left during his second year when he was seventeen because he had become too busy getting into business. He spent three years building up two successful companies before concentrating on his first love – music.

Chris's dad, Bob, was an accountant by trade, but had always dabbled in the music business. His first big step into mainstream pop had come in the mid 1980s when he was introduced to Chris's best friends from Collingwood School in Camberley, Surrey. They were the twins Matt and Luke Goss, who had their own pop group called Gloss together with another boy, Craig Logan. The boys were only fifteen, but Bob saw their potential and became their manager. He let them practise in his summer house, introduced them to songwriters, paid for their earliest demo tapes and planned their route to a record deal. Bob couldn't sign the boys on a contract until they were eighteen, but, just as they reached that birthday, the unthinkable happened and they were signed by another established record producer and Bob lost control. It was a devastating blow; the boys became Bros, the hugely successful money-spinning group of the late 1980s.

Despite that galling disappointment, Bob continued with music management, albeit with lower profile acts, until his son Chris became his partner. During the autumn of 1993, one of Bob's wealthy business contacts, a colourful cockney called Chic Murphy, said he wanted to invest in a new project. Chic, a heavy-set man in his 50s with swept-back grey hair, had made millions through varying ventures from selling cars and luxury yachts, to professional gambling. He scooped vast sums at the gaming tables and poker – in one game alone he won a house – and now the high-roller was ready for a punt in the pop game.

Chic wasn't new to music. He had managed successful artists such as the 1950s American group the Platters and the 1970s female line-up, the Three Degrees. He had taken on both groups in their decline but prolonged their success with lucrative tours on the British cabaret circuit, making thousands by selling signed records at the venues.

In light of Take That's success, Bob and Chic planned to start a boy band, but Chris was one major step ahead – he thought they should start a girl group instead. Girl bands weren't new, but all attempts to recreate the success of Bananarama in the 1980s had failed. The key factor hindering girl groups was the lack of support from teen magazines, which knew that girl readers saw them as a threat to their relationships with their own boyfriends. The only group which seemed to be breaking through was Eternal, who had reached No. 4 with their début single, 'Stay', in October 1993.

But Chris's idea for his group would create a new mould and succeed where the others failed. He wanted his girls to be street-wise, full of attitude and have a mix of characters which young girls would identify with. The bonus to this group would be its appeal to the army of boys who were neglected by the obsession with boy bands. It took a while for Chris to convince his father and Chic that the group would work. Even when they had warmed to the idea, Chic, the man who would finance the project, wanted initially to fly in long-legged black girls from America and recreate the Three Degrees. Finally though, Chic and Bob agreed with the young man's plan, and the long hunt for who would eventually become the Spice Girls began.

Chris went to work immediately and began his search in the weeks leading up to Christmas. His first step was to get a thousand postcard-size flyers printed. He designed a Wild-West-style WANTED scroll and thought long and hard before he wrote the advert itself. He zeroed in on exactly the type of *characters* he wanted, not the look or background; and came up with four key words to sum up his ideal group member: streetwise, outgoing, ambitious and dedicated. Chris wanted raw girls, not models with cat-walk figures.

For the next two months, Chris never stopped thinking about the group. The image and balance of the line-up came ever more sharply into focus as he clocked up thousands of miles driving around London, the South-east and the major cities in the Midlands and the North, including Birmingham, Manchester and Liverpool. He visited the key dance and drama schools in those cities, put up his flyers on notice boards and handed them out to girls, asking them to send in their CVs and portfolios if they were interested in being in his group. Even in the street while out shopping, or in the pub while he was with his girlfriend, Chris never stopped looking. If a girl caught his attention, he stopped her, explained what he was doing and gave her a flyer.

In London, he hung out at big dance studios such as Pineapple and Dance Works and he scoured the *Stage* for audition adverts. He went along to auditions for West End shows and would sit at the back of a studio and carefully watch each girl, sizing up her look and attitude, then approach the ones he liked at the stage door on their way out. At times, he got funny looks for loitering around, but soon had a captive audience once he revealed why he was there. The girls he was talking to were hungry for fame, so they were instantly interested.

By the end of January, Chris was exhausted. He had handed out all the cards and the replies had flooded into the office he shared with his dad in a house converted into a business centre in a Surrey village. It was only a cramped upstairs room – not a designer deco-rated office in London like the big record companies have – but it was functional and it was where the next stage of the spice trail took place. Chris and Bob sifted through hundreds of photos of young faces dreaming of stardom and examined carefully typed CVs. Slowly, the mass of paperwork was honed to a manageable size, then the process started again until they had a concentrated top-eighty 'short list' of the best. Those girls were then contacted and invited to an audition.

Chris had a gut feeling that eighty girls might not be enough to produce the exact five girls he needed, so, at the last minute he decided to throw the audition open to everyone. On 24 February, he placed a modified version of the 'WANTED' flyers in an advert in the *Stage* inviting girls to an open audition for the group. It was a fateful decision because, if it hadn't been for this ad, the driving force behind the Spice Girls might never have been discovered.

~

As the clock struck 11am, Chris prepared to find the stars of the future among the line of dreamers down those stairs. The studio was booked for six and a half hours, so it was going to be an exhausting day. The girls were put into groups of ten and then asked to dance to Eternal's 'Stay' as if they were in a nightclub. Chris wanted to see their natural rhythm and ideas, not carefully memo-rised choreographed steps.

The judging was done rather like a boxing bout with four people giving scores – Chris, Bob, a friend called Sarah Davison who was a dancer and choreographer, and Chris's girlfriend, Shelley D'Silva, who had been a stylist for many pop groups. They all gave each girl a score out of ten in several categories, including their dance ability, looks and personality. Group after group came in and danced and, as the hours ticked by, the boxes on the judges' A4 pads slowly filled up. The girls with the best all-round marks were then asked to wait outside for the next stage of the audition.

As the afternoon wore on, the second phase began where the best girls were brought back to sing a song of their choice. A small PA system had been set up, so they sang into a microphone on a stand either to a backing tape they had brought, or to a piano accompaniment. A video camera on a tripod filmed their performance. The singing section helped the judges narrow their selections to around twenty and it was here that three of the girls who would become Spice Girls were spotted.

Melanie Chisholm was particularly impressive thanks to her strong, soulful voice. She was also full of confidence and grabbed the microphone out of its stand to belt out 'I'm So Excited' by the Pointer Sisters. Dressed in a T-shirt and dark trousers, with her shoulder-length hair loose, Mel moved her free hand animatedly and danced as she sang. She was so happy with her performance, she gave the judges a cheeky nod as she left.

Melanie Brown's effort was a complete contrast. She had gone to Dance Works that day to audition for a performing job on a six-month cruise. A friend she met there was going for the pop group trial and suggested Mel give it a go. She wasn't keen at first but something told her it was worth a try. The last-minute decision may have accounted for her nerves because she stood stiffly and her voice trembled out of tune as she sang Whitney Houston's 'Greatest Love of All'. Despite her obvious nerves, the Herberts liked her looks and personality.

Another girl who made a good impression, but for different reasons, was Victoria Adams. She sang 'Mein Herr', a song from the movie and stage show *Cabaret*. She was slightly cocky and theatrically thrusted her pelvis and threw back her head as she sang. She also came across a bit aloof and sophisticated, but the judges liked that side to her character.

A fter a long day at Dance Works, Chris and Bob finally packed up the equipment and headed home. They were pleased with the turn-out and instinctively knew there was some potential hidden in the reams of video footage and mass of scores in their pads. They were realistic and knew they had a long way to go before their idea would start taking shape.

As for the girls who gave it their best shot that day: some were low with disappointment from their performance, most wrote it off as just another lousy audition among dozens in their pursuit of fame, but many went home hoping and praying they were still in with a chance.

– 2 –

LADY OF
THE DANCE

VICTORIA'S STORY

Victoria Adams had been a professionally trained dancer since she was a little girl, so it was no wonder she had jazzed up her audition with some stage glitz. Victoria was born on 7 April 1975 and from her earliest years her head was filled with dreams of becoming a star. She was a natural attention seeker and show off, who would dance around the house for her family and friends. She loved dancing so much that when she was eight, her mum finally decided to encourage her daughter's passion and took her to a dance school.

Joy Spriggs, who owns the Jason Theatre School, remembered that day well. 'Her mum told me that Victoria was mad about dancing and she wanted to know if she had any real talent. As soon as I watched Victoria dance, I knew she was special. She had natural ability and a very lively personality. Even as a little girl she already had the instinctive movements of dance. She needed to be trained properly, but I could tell she had rhythm and I knew we could draw her talent out.'

Much of Victoria's desire for performing may have come from her dad, Tony, who had been in a group in the 1960s called the Sonics. The group had shown some promise, but he gave up his dreams of pop stardom to marry Victoria's mum, Jackie. The couple went into business and spent years building up a lucrative electrical goods wholesale dealership. Success allowed them to afford a large country home with a swimming pool in Goff's Oak, Hertfordshire, and a Rolls Royce for Tony. The money provided Victoria and her younger brother and sister, Louise and Christian, with a secure and privileged childhood, with regular family holidays abroad and all the material things many children long for.

Victoria's main indulgence was her dancing lessons at Jason Theatre School, twenty-five minutes away in Broxbourne. In the beginning, she was driven there twice a week by her mum after a day at primary school. She was coached in all modes of dancing, from tap and ballet, to jazz and modern, and had singing lessons, too. The school had around 300 pupils in all and Victoria enrolled in a class of about twenty-five girls, plus a few boys. She was a bit of an outsider because most of the pupils lived locally, but that didn't worry her. Victoria loved every minute and was a noticeably quick learner with lots of confidence. She had a deep desire to perform and soon shone out above the others. Joy Spriggs always tried not to separate her pupils by giving one more credit than the rest, but she admitted that Victoria was among three girls who were way ahead of their contemporaries – and was keen to show it. 'I could always guarantee I would find Victoria near the front of the class,' said Mrs Spriggs. 'She had a natural way of getting noticed and was quicker to learn dance steps than many of the other children. It would be wrong to say she was *the* best, but she certainly was one of them in her class.'

The Jason Theatre School traditionally holds an annual show under the umbrella title 'Let Us Entertain You'. It's not a full-length production of one show, but more of a variety mix for the parents and Broxbourne residents. Pupils from all age-groups are involved, whether in singing or dancing solos, or just as part of a group section. Victoria's first part which could be loosely described as a 'starring role' came when she was nine. That year's show included a piece from 'The Emperor's New Clothes', the fairytale about the Emperor who is conned into wearing an invisible outfit. Victoria was the little boy who speaks the truth and shouts out that he has no clothes on. It was a big moment for young Victoria. Mrs Spriggs said, 'She had a couple of lines to say and that was her first speaking part with us. I don't remember her being particularly nervous, but she would have been very excited. She enjoyed herself and did very well.'

From her début solo spot, Victoria progressed to bigger parts. In one show she performed a tap dancing duet with another girl. They both wore pinks leotards, gloves and large pink bow-ties, with black top-hats and canes. By the time she was twelve, Victoria had mastered many routines in different dancing styles and was a shining talent at the school. She was spotted by the local amateur dramatic society and was one of the lucky few to be selected for its shows at the Broxbourne Civic Theatre. She appeared as a tap dancing munchkin in *The Wizard of Oz* and also in a production of *Hello Dolly*.

In photos from those exciting days as a young performer, Victoria was a natural for the camera and clearly relished dressing up and dancing. But there is one big difference from that sweet child and the sour-faced poses the world would associate with Posh Spice – the enchanting smile. Back when she was an uninhibited young girl, Victoria smiled readily and wasn't self-conscious about the obvious gap between her front teeth. It was only as she grew older that she would begin to worry about it and as vanity took over in her teenage years, she began to tighten her smile for professional pictures. Even when the gap was corrected years later, she didn't revert to the innocent toothy grin. Eventually, her performer's pose would develop into a tight-lipped scowl and become her celebrity trademark.

Another reason Victoria's smile began to vanish when she was a teenager was the problems she experienced at school. She had enjoyed going to the local infant and primary schools, where she had appeared in many productions such as *The Pied Piper*. But away from the stage she was a quiet and shy girl who got on with her work and didn't mix well with her classmates. She had a few selected close friends, but she never became part of the big crowd who hung out together after school because dance lessons dominated her free time. Not being part of the gang didn't bother Victoria because she was happy to do her schoolwork and go dancing.

But the climate changed when she went to senior school. Teenagers are less forgiving of those who don't want to be in the gang, and it wasn't long before Victoria found herself the target of bullying. It was confusing because she had never outwardly offended anyone, or behaved differently; it was simply that she refused to be part of the gang and the others construed that as her being aloof. While the 'cool' girls were smoking in the bike sheds, Victoria was in the classroom swotting for a test or doing home-work. After school, the gang would hang out at the local shops flirting with boys, while Victoria went to dance school. Even if she had wanted to be with the gang, her mum wouldn't have let her. Jackie Adams wanted her daughter to have worthwhile interests and a wider perspective on life.

Basically, Victoria was seen as a goody-goody for never getting into trouble and a prima donna because of her dancing. Matters were made worse because she also came from a wealthy family, and the fact that her dad drove a Rolls Royce more or less sealed her fate. Victoria used to squirm with embarrassment as her dad dropped her and her brother and sister off at school in the Roller because she knew the problems it would cause. She would beg him to drive the van instead, but most days he needed the car for business. The bullying began with name calling and escalated to mental intimidation, but she was never physically beaten up. They called her 'Acne Face' because of teenage spots and ridiculed her ski-jump-shaped nose. The names were cruel and the threats of violence were frightening.

The experience cast a disturbing shadow over her entire senior school years and had a lasting impact on Victoria. Years later, when she had made it with the Spice Girls, she told *Sugar* magazine, 'I never had lots of friends at school; if anything, I was the least popular and I hated it. What really used to get me was that I never really asked for trouble. They picked on me because I used to work very hard at school. I was an outsider. I never used to swear or anything like that, so I was uncool. It was uncool to come from a nice family, work hard and be polite.

'I remember I'd go to classes and be petrified. I'd usually get pushed around and sworn at and then the girls who did it would say things like, "We're gonna get you after school." Later on, they'd all be standing there waiting for me at the school gates, pushing me around. They never actually beat me up, but that's irrelevant. It was the waiting for things to happen that was torture.'

As the bullying continued at school, Victoria looked forward even more to the dancing lessons. It didn't matter that she wasn't one of the Broxbourne kids because she was there to dance. She would lose herself in the ballet or jazz lessons, listening intently to the music and concentrating on the complicated steps. The frustrations and hurt of the intimidation by the bullies would ebb away with the exertions of dancing.

Victoria's parents were keen to encourage her dancing and, luckily, they had the resources to pay for extra lessons as her childhood pastime became more serious. By the time she was fourteen, Victoria was going to classes three or four times a week. She was also given whatever she needed, whether it was new dance shoes, new leggings or leotards, or a tape player for music. Victoria would probably be the first to agree that she was spoilt, but it would prove to be money well spent. Joy Spriggs added, 'Victoria lived, ate, slept and drank dancing. I saw her dedication and it made me think, This girl really has got something. Like all the girls who go to dance school, she had stars in her eyes. She danced instinctively and she loved performing. She also had a nice singing voice, which had an unusual, catchy sound. It's difficult to describe the sound, but if I closed my eyes I would always be able to pick out her voice amongst the other pupils.

'After a while it was obvious dance was more than just a hobby for Victoria. She really started to see that it was something she wanted to pursue as a career. We have a careers teacher at the school and Victoria told her she wanted to go into the theatre. She wanted to be in the big West End musicals.

'Her mum encouraged her all the way. She wasn't pushy, but was always there to help. I used to chat to her about Victoria's future and the options she had in front of her. Victoria was lucky because it's expensive to have lessons over a period of years, but her family were able to afford them.'

Victoria finally made the decision to follow a career in showbusiness, no matter how risky it would be, rather than continue with academic schooling. She had to step up the work rate to qualify for a good stage school. Such schools hold entrance exams as tough as auditions for professional shows. She started going to the Jason Theatre every night and would practice for hours at weekends. But her dedication paid off quickly and Victoria excelled at the dance school and won three special awards – the Senior Choreographic Award, the Shakespeare Shield for drama, and the Personality Cup.

When she was fifteen, Victoria's father installed a new alarm system at the house. The young man sent to fit it was Mark Wood, a nineteen-year-old security consultant. As he worked around the sprawling house, he got chatting to Victoria and was instantly smitten. Mark was so infatuated he went back to the house several times on the pretence of checking the alarm, even though he knew it was working fine. He was so determined to go out with Victoria he ended a relationship he was already in before he knew for sure she liked him. Sometimes Mark would turn up at the house unexpectedly, only to be told by her mum that Victoria was out. He would later discover that on these occasions she'd hidden because she thought she wasn't dressed nicely enough to make a good impression.

Finally, after a short period of playing games, Mark plucked up the courage to phone Victoria and ask her out. She said yes and he took her to a wine bar. It was one of her first serious dates and she was very nervous, particularly as Mark was so much older. She was also new to drinking alcohol and the mix of nerves and immaturity with booze made a heady cocktail and she proceeded to get very drunk. By the time he had finished paying for her first Bacardi and Coke, she had gulped it down. During the night, Victoria became progressively giggly, but Mark was charmed by her girlie innocence.

It was the beginning of a five-and-a-half-year romance, which became serious quite quickly. Little more than six months into the relationship, Victoria, now sixteen, lost her virginity to Mark at her house while her parents were away. Her mum was opened-minded and Victoria had spoken to her about it beforehand. The relationship intensified and Mark became very possessive, but, as a girl who was used to getting her own way, Victoria loved having an extra person to pander to her wishes.

The happiness of her first love was soon turned upside down when she won a place at one of the country's top dance and drama colleges. It was a bitter-sweet triumph because it meant moving away and leaving her family and Mark. But she had done well to pass the entry exams for a three-year course at the Laine Theatre Arts School in Surrey. It was an opportunity she had been dreaming of and working towards, so there was no question that she would go for it.

Victoria moved into the school's hall of residence and at first she hated it. She missed Mark and her family very badly and found it hard to cope with the bitchiness of some girls. Victoria had gone on the Pill shortly before joining the school and it had made her put on weight. She had always been slightly heavy throughout her teen years, but it had been kept down because of her dancing. But even the rigorous training at Laine wasn't enough to keep her from piling on the pounds. The other girls came out with cruel remarks about her figure, so she decided to come off the Pill and get her weight under control.

Even with her weight down, Victoria received lots of criticism about her look and ability in that first year, and she found it hard to take. She had come from being the star of her dance school, who was praised for everything, to being one of the middle order in a ferociously competitive atmosphere. It was a shock and she was so upset she constantly reached for the phone in tears to Mark or her mum. In hour-long chats, she would sob and say how much she missed the security and luxury of home. She got so homesick on some evenings, she would head home and return to Laine in the early hours.

Whatever the hardships at Laine, it toughened Victoria up and did her nothing but good. And she needed to be tough if she was serious about following a career in the brutal world of theatre. The teachers at Laine wanted to prepare her for the countless knocks she would face along the way. She had to develop a thick skin to deflect recurring rejection and, during her three years away from the comfort of Goff's Oak, Victoria started to grow up.

During the first year, she had some professional photos taken for her portfolio by local photographer Geoff Marchant. She paid him £25 and insisted on moody black-and-white photographs. She was certainly a girl who knew what she wanted and it was one of the first indications that she was determined to keep her smile sealed. Geoff revealed, 'Many of the youngsters I work with just turn up and ask me what I want them to do. But Toria directed me, which isn't something you'd expect from most sixteen-year-olds. She knew just what she wanted. She wouldn't have any smiling shots, they were all serious. At one stage I told her she needed at least a couple of smiling pictures in her portfolio, but she wanted them all to look moody.'

There were things to smile about for Victoria in the second year at Laine when her parents bought her a flat. It was a large two-bedroom place and several girls from her class moved in with her. She enjoyed the freedom of living there and it meant Mark was able to stay. Their relationship was as strong as ever and when she was on holiday from college, they would always be together. Mark got on well with her parents, so they had the run of the Adams' lovely home as well and went on holidays together to her parents' villa in Southern Spain. They went on skiing holidays in the winter and partied at extravagant balls in the summer. Mark was accepted as one of the family and even moved into the Adams' house.

Victoria passed all her exams at Laine and left full of hope for the future. She struggled initially and was rejected at many auditions, but then she got her first big break when she landed a part as a chorus-line dancer in a show called *Bertie*, in Birmingham. It was great news, although she was upset it meant being away from Mark for three months. In fact, she was so concerned she suggested a dramatic measure to keep the relationship secure in her absence – she wanted to get engaged!

At first, Mark wasn't sure it was the right move, but he warmed to the idea, and went through the formal procedure of asking her dad's permission. Tony and Jackie were delighted and laid on a lavish garden party to celebrate. To top the celebrations, Mark paid £1,500 for a specially made engagement ring. Sadly, despite all the dreams of being together forever, the relationship would be doomed by Victoria's ambition.

Victoria enjoyed the thrill of being in *Bertie*, but that first triumph was swiftly followed by a depressing drought with nothing but rejections. It was the harsh, all too familiar reality of the childhood dream of stardom. She went for many auditions and had a few recalls, but Victoria couldn't get another job. She would lie about her age, height and experience in the vain hope of getting another break, but it didn't help and slowly her confidence drained. She had tried to build a tough exterior, but the rejection hurt like hell. She managed to keep busy by doing promotion work at hairdressing and fashion shows, and she modelled for make-up companies. She even got some work with Sky Television during their coverage of the Rugby World Cup. But it was all a long way from the fantasy of taking centre stage in a West End musical.

Things started to change when she saw an advert for a new pop group, which was being put together by a musician called Steve Andrews. He wanted a five-piece group of three girls, himself and another guy. Steve would manage and develop the group until they got a recording contract. Victoria sent off her favourite picture from her portfolio – one of her all in black, with fishnet stockings, gloves and dark glasses, pouting provocatively to the camera. Steve said, 'I had hundreds of applications, but as soon as I saw Victoria's picture I knew I had to offer her a place. She looked sexy in the photo. It was just the image I was looking for. Her CV said she had been to drama school, but hadn't sung professionally. I didn't care – I wanted to see her in the flesh. My feeling was right. She walked into the room and looked great. She was a shy, mummy's girl but that was half the attraction. She wasn't a great singer, but she had potential and I knew I had found the right girl. She was hungry for fame and willing to work hard.'

Steve gave Victoria the job and, once he had made his other selections, they called themselves Persuasion and started rehearsals. Victoria tried hard, but her voice shook with nerves when she sang into a microphone in those early days. Another downside was that Mark was so possessive he would often come to rehearsals which created a bad atmosphere. Despite the early problems, Persuasion worked together for many months and gradually developed into a tight group with some potential.

Steve didn't realise that Victoria was keeping her eyes open for other opportunities. It was during this time she went for the Dance Works audition and the talent spotters there also saw the star potential in Victoria Adams.

– 3 –

FRIENDS FROM THE NORTH

A TALE OF TWO MELS

Chris and Bob Herbert continued to examine the video footage from Dance Works and gradually whittled down the numbers. They had the hours of tapes edited into a manageable cassette and then started their deliberations again with Shelley and Sarah. They kept coming back to the two Mels – Brown and Chisholm. Although very different in looks and ability, they both showed tremendous character and their Northern backgrounds would give the group diversity.

Melanie Jayne Chisholm was from Liverpool. She was born on 12 January 1974 and was brought up in a smart semi-detached house. Her dad, Alan, was a manager at a travel firm and her mum, Joan, was a secretary for a local council authority. Mel was an only child and was always a bright and energetic little girl, but, sadly, her early childhood was troubled by the deep-rooted problems in her parents' marriage. Alan and Joan were having difficulties and no matter how hard they tried, they had to accept their marriage was doomed. When Mel was seven, the couple finally decided to separate.

It was a hard situation for Mel to understand and accept and she would simply say later, 'I think I was a bit too upset to talk about it and a bit confused.'

Mel stayed with her mum and they moved out of the family house to live in Widnes, Cheshire. They moved in with Joan's boyfriend, a taxi driver called Den O'Neil and, a few years later, Mel's half-brother, Paul, was born. Having a fragmented family must have continued to present its problems over the years, but Mel stayed in touch and as close as possible to her real dad, albeit at a distance. One positive outcome was that it brought two older step-brothers on Den's side and later, when her dad remarried, Mel would have two younger half-brothers.

Mel settled into life in Widnes and went to the local school, Fairfield County High. She had always shown an interest in dance and acting as a young girl and this interest grew stronger at Fairfield. She was deeply involved in drama and would appear in school plays and she also developed a strong singing voice. Her singing and desire to perform was undoubtedly inherited from her mum, who was the passionate lead singer of a cabaret group called T-Junction. The group played mainly a set of cover versions at social clubs around the area and other small venues in the North. Joan was known for strong vocals, particularly her raunchy Tina Turner routines, and T-Junction built up a modest reputation on the club circuit. Years later, however, that reputation would soar thanks to Mel's fame in the Spice Girls; suddenly, Joan was a star, too, and T-Junction would become overwhelmed with bookings.

In the long run Mel's pop star ambitions may have come from watching her mum in the clubs, but as a teenager her main dreams were in theatre and dance. Although she would cultivate a football-mad tomboy image in the Spice Girls, back then she was very different. She was a school prefect and, contrary to her current image, Mel was a proper little lady who loved ballet and was also very popular with the boys.

Mark Deany, a friend at Fairfield, remembered, 'She was always very girlie. She was ballet mad and wasn't into football. Mel was well liked and all the boys fancied her, but she was never sexy and outrageous like the Spice Girls. She was very quiet and always played the good girl. No one can believe she's ended up as a Spice Girl.'

Mel pursued her love of acting and singing and played one of the old crows in a production of *The Wiz*, a modern musical based on *The Wizard of Oz*. One of her best performances at school was starring in *Blood Brothers,* and during rehearsals for this show she fell for her co-star, Ian McKnight. They went out together for a few months, but Ian finally dumped her. Mel was so upset she tried to get her own back by going out with Ian's younger brother, Keith, a year younger than her, but that relationship also ended quickly.

Mel soon put the mess of going out with the McKnight brothers behind her and, when she was fifteen, she started dating Ryan Wilson, who was in her class. Ryan was certainly pleased to have Mel as his girlfriend because, as he puts it, she was 'a cut above, a real lady' and lots of the other boys fancied her. It developed into Mel's first serious relationship and, after six months together, they made love for the first time. Mel recalled later, 'I lost my virginity when I was sixteen and it was incredibly romantic. We did it while his parents were away so we could spend the whole night together. It was wonderful.'

Mel and Ryan were together for almost two years, but finally split up because Mel had to leave Widnes to go to drama college. It was her dream to be a star of the stage and she went for many auditions for various schools. She was thrilled when she landed a place at the respected Doreen Bird Dance School. She had performed a piece from *Blood Brothers* for her audition and the notes taken at the time emerged years later. They read, 'Mel has a nice appeal. She is strong, with a flexible body. Her audition piece was very nice. She is bright and has good potential. Should do well.'

The Doreen Bird school is in Sidcup, Kent, hundreds of miles away from Widnes, so it would have been difficult for Mel to continue going out with Ryan, but it was a sacrifice she was happy to make. She moved down to Kent and quickly asserted herself as a hard-working and determined pupil. She was dedicated to becoming the best and revealed at the time that her main ambition was to star in the West End musical *Cats*. She also told her teachers of another dream – to make a record. Pat Izen, the school's musical director, said, 'Melanie didn't have a particularly good voice when she arrived – it was gutsy, but she was a real individualist and always stuck out for what she wanted.'

Mel worked hard at Doreen Bird and passed her exams, but, like Victoria, it wasn't enough to secure her dreams of West End stardom. Mel went for many auditions and was good enough to get recalled several times. At one stage she was even down to the last few for a good part in *Cats*, but then lost out. It was a crushing disappointment, but the gutsy side to her character, which had shone through at Doreen Bird, helped her carry on trying. Mel signed on the dole and continued to live in Sidcup in a sparse flat with friends. She enjoyed a student lifestyle of wild parties and nightclubbing, while taking whatever work she could get. Gradually, her hopes of that starring role faded and she began to focus on her other ambition – to make a record. Then she heard about the men searching for a pop group.

~

Melanie Janine Brown had taken a similar, but more varied path to the Dance Works audition. She was born on 29 May 1975 to Martin and Andrea Brown, a couple who had faced some racial problems over their mixed-raced marriage. Martin was originally from the tiny Caribbean island Nevis, where Mel's grandmother and other relatives still live. Martin was a night-shift worker at a local engineering factory and did long hours to provide a comfortable home for his family. They lived in a modest semi-detached house in the Burley area of Leeds. It was a world away from Victoria's mansion with its pool; Mel's dad was more used to going to work on an old racing bike than a Rolls Royce. Money may have been tight at times in the Brown household, but Mel and her sister Danielle, who is five years younger, had a happy childhood.

Like the other girls, Mel was a precocious young performer who was always eager to grab the attention. She got involved in her infant school plays and took ballet lessons and always seemed to be ahead of the other girls, particularly at dancing. She had natural rhythm and a lot of confidence for a young girl and it led her to join a community dance group. She was only eleven and the class was made up of much older children and some adults, but Mel wasn't intimidated. She had far too much belief in her own ability to worry about anyone else.

The dance lessons helped her progress and made her realise she wanted to pursue a career in dance and music. Her parents fully supported her and when she was thirteen she went to Intake High School, which was the only school in the area offering a worthwhile performing arts course. The head of that department was David Robbins, who had played music at Mel's community dance group. He had already been impressed with her ability and dedication in those lessons and when he had to interview her for a place at Intake, it was already certain that she would be accepted.

Mel appeared in many productions at the school, including *Jesus Christ Superstar*. She didn't have a starring role, but was given a gospel song to sing because of her strong, deep voice. During her three years at Intake, Mr Robbins witnessed the strength of character which would help Mel secure her place as a Spice Girl. Even then, she was a loud girl, who told people exactly what she thought and never backed down in an argument. She also had a fiercely ambitious streak. Mr Robbins revealed, 'She was very confident, extremely competitive and was never frightened to speak her mind. She would always try to get the last word in a dispute. But it's that kind of trait which has helped her get where she is. It struck me then that at some point in her life this girl was going to make it big. Mel knew, too. She'd say her ambition was to be famous – she wanted to be a star. You can tell the children who want fame badly enough and Mel was one of those children. Some people perform when they have to, but she loved being on stage and having an audience.'

Mr Robbins also taught Mel how to write pop songs during her GCSE music course. He outlined the basic three-minute formula and standard structure and Mel completed two songs, which went towards her final exam grade – an exam she passed. At this time, Mel also started having lessons on the drums, an instrument which suited her character perfectly – loud, expressive and full of energy. She loved playing them so much she would drive her family mad with her incessant practising at home. She couldn't afford a drum kit but she bought a pair of drum sticks and improvised by playing a beat on every solid object and surface around the house.

Mel was always a headstrong girl who would do whatever she wanted. She also had an infectious enthusiasm in everything she did and a constant desire to be different. This came through in her dress sense. As a teenager, she wore bright colours and had a keen eye for the latest street trends. She even added little touches to her school uniform to make it look more stylish.

Her mixed-race background also gave her a more open view on life. When she was young she believed she had the surname Brown because of the colour of her skin. She suffered some racial taunts, but she grew to be able to see both sides of the racial divide and, thanks to her parents, it made her blind to colour. Mel revealed to *Pride* magazine, 'I don't see myself as black. I don't see myself as white. I'm mixed, completely mixed, which means I've got the best of both worlds. When I meet anyone I don't see colour, I'm just me. I don't even think it should be an issue to talk about really, even though unfortunately you still have prejudice and you still have racism. I don't feel as though I have to put on a black thing or a white thing or do anything else apart from just be myself. I had loads of mixed-raced friends that I went to school with and I had a lot of black male friends as well, so it was all right. Whenever I used to have problems, I'd go to my dad for one side and go to my mum for another side.'

After leaving Intake High School, Mel enrolled for a two-year course at Leeds College of Music, where she steadily became an accomplished drummer and she also studied at the Northern School of Contemporary Dance. A party animal, Mel loved the nightclubbing scene of Leeds and would move from one club to the next dancing for hours on end through the night. At one stage, she used to earn extra money by dancing in a bikini on a podium for £3 an hour at the Yel Club. She was certainly a striking seventeen-year-old and it helped her win the Miss Leeds Weekly News beauty contest. The first prize was a Renault Clio for a year – even though she hadn't passed her test yet – and a weekend for two in Paris, plus a modelling course. Not a bad result from her first competition of that kind.

It was during a night on the town that Mel met one of her first serious boyfriends, Steve Mulrain, who was an apprentice footballer with Leeds United. He had fancied Mel the moment he saw her in the Gallery nightclub. They only met fleetingly that night, but he couldn't get her out of his mind, so he kept going back to the club over the next two months until he saw her again. He then wasted no time in asking her out. The couple hit it off immediately. Apart from a physical attraction, they also shared a mutual ambition to succeed in their chosen careers. It was the beginning of a passionate fling. They spent most nights together, but then Mel got a dancing job for the summer season in Blackpool. Steve missed her so much he travelled there every weekend to stay in a house she was sharing with a group of other dancers.

Sadly, Mel finished the relationship when she had to move to London after being accepted for the *Starlight Express* trainee roller-skating school. During her time in London she went to many fruitless auditions and started to realise just how tough it was to make a living as a dancer. She was becoming disillusioned with that world when her mum suggested she try becoming a singer instead. Mel liked the idea and started having lessons. While down in London, she bumped into Melanie Chisholm many times on the audition circuit and they became good friends. The girls had a lot in common and talked of those childhood dreams of starring in musicals which had faded into disappointment and frustration. They had made quite different journeys from the North, but the two Mels had ended up at the same destination and soon their lives would be entwined in a common dream.

~

Chris and Bob Herbert and the other judges spent the best part of six weeks analysing the candidates on the video. They discussed each girl's strong points, weak areas and how certain characters could blend together in a group. It was an agonisingly slow process, but finally they selected nine girls. Among them were the two Mels and Victoria, four from various parts of the North of England and one from Cardiff, Wales. The ninth person was Michelle Stephenson, a college student and talented performer from

Abingdon, Oxfordshire. All the girls were invited to a second and final audition to be held on 17 May at NOMIS, a well-known studio and rehearsal complex in West London, so named because it was the original owner's first name spelt backwards.

Shortly before the second audition the phone rang at the Herberts' office. It was a girl who had been unable to make it to the open audition, but was desperate to be in the group. Chris explained how far down the line they were with selecting the group and that there was no real point auditioning her. They had already rejected dozens of talented girls, so why on earth would they want a wild card now. His gut reaction had been that if someone wanted to be in the group badly enough, they would have made the effort to come to the first audition. But, as he listened to the determined sales pitch from the girl, he began to admire her cheek. Before he knew it, he was writing her name down as the tenth girl for NOMIS.

Chris could be forgiven if he came off the phone slightly bedazzled. After all, he had just been introduced to the world of Geri Halliwell and Girl Power.

– 4 –

NAKED
AMBITION

GERI'S STORY

Anyone who knew Geri Halliwell wouldn't have been remotely surprised by the barefaced cheek of her call to the Herberts. Nor would they have been amazed she had pulled off what most girls in the same position would think impossible. Geri had always been a quick-witted chancer with the gift of the gab to get round anyone when she wanted something. To her, the answer 'No' simply didn't exist.

Geri would admit later that if she had gone to that first audition she would probably not have been chosen because she wasn't a trained dancer or singer. Her defining features were her character and driving ambition, which would have been smothered in the throng of lithe dancers withgood voices.

But Geri must have smiled to herself after she won Chris round for she knew her chances were pretty good in a group of ten because it was a playing field she could tilt to her advantage by imposing her personality.

Ironically, the same spirited determination which carried Geri effortlessly into the second round would prove to be the critical inspiration for the success of the Spice Girls.

It's no wonder Geri was such a determined young woman. Both her parents were strong-minded individuals. Her dad was Liverpool-born Lawrence Halliwell, whose family moved to London when he was a boy. Lawrence was a naturally streetwise wheeler-dealer who could think on his feet and, after serving in the RAF during the war, he became a successful car salesman. His first marriage ended in divorce, but, when he was forty-four, he fell in love with Anna Hildago, a pretty eighteen-year-old Spanish girl who was working as an au pair. Anna had left her large family in Northern Spain to seek adventure in England. It was rare in the 1960s for such a young girl to break with tradition in Spain, but, like Lawrence, Anna was a free spirit who wanted excitement in life.

Soon after marrying, the couple had a son, Max, and two years later he was followed by Natalie. Then, on 6 August 1972, Geraldine Estelle, their third and last child was born, not long before her father's fiftieth birthday.

Geri's early years were fairly unremarkable. She was a normal fun-loving little girl who grew up in a happy home in Watford, Hertfordshire. She got on well with her brother and sister and was a diligent pupil at her local primary school. She worked hard and earnt herself a place at Watford Grammar School for Girls. Unlike the two Mels and Victoria, Geri wasn't driven in her earliest years by a burning desire to sing and dance. She did have an early introduction to strong women singers by her dad who always filled the house with the hits of the Supremes and the Three Degrees. She would make him laugh by performing skits of these great artists, but there were no ballet and tap lessons for young Geri.

The Halliwell children had a wonderful extended family in Spain and they went on many holidays to their mum's hometown of Huesca, in the foothills of the Pyrenees. They would stay at her aunt Maria's home and Geri enjoyed getting to know the Spanish culture and learning the language. As an eight-year-old, she would dress up in traditional costumes, complete with Spanish-style scraped-back hair and dangly earrings. She would look like a little doll in her outfit and was pampered by her Spanish relatives, but she was always so tiny for her age that it earnt her the nickname La Enana, Spanish for 'the dwarf'.

On these holidays, Geri was allowed to stay up late during local fiestas and loved the fun of dancing and singing with the adults. But the one part of the Spanish culture she hated was bullfights and whenever she was taken to one she would cry and wish she could take the bull home and look after him. Although she was sensitive to animals, there was a tough side to Geri, even as a child; and it was something her aunt Maria noticed. Maria said, 'Geri is just like me – a rebel who needs a firm hand. She has a fiery temper. We are both explosive and impulsive and we rowed from the moment she was big enough to sit on my knee. She is like a pineapple – soft and sweet on the inside, but with a tough exterior for the outside world.

'She was a big hit with the local boys when she got older because she was blonde and foreign, but I made sure she didn't get into trouble. It didn't make me very popular with Geri. She'd call me a pig and I'd call her one.'

The happy Halliwell household was thrown into turmoil when Lawrence and Anna's marriage hit the rocks. The vast age gap between them finally proved too great an obstacle. Geri was ten at the time and it was a traumatic time for her and her brother and sister. To spare the children some of the emotional problems, they were sent to live with close friends locally while their parents settled the separation. Finally, they came back to live with their mum, while Lawrence moved into a flat just two miles away. The split meant Geri's mum had to work, which in turn led to Geri becoming a very independent young girl. Even though she was the baby of the family, she grew used to getting herself to school and generally looking after herself while her mum worked long hours.

Although, her dad was no longer a daily feature in Geri's life, the separation actually brought them closer. Then in his sixties, Lawrence had taken the foot off the pedal in business and enjoyed a slower pace of life. Geri would go round to his house after school and, at weekends, they would spend hours on his main hobby, hunting for bric-a-brac at car boot fairs. Lawrence saw a lot of himself in Geri and a deep bond developed between them. Her energy and cheeky character were a joy to him and he loved her spirit of adventure.

It was during this period that Lawrence instilled in Geri an attitude to life which would have a lasting impact on her. One day, when she was eleven or twelve, he saw her upset after some girls had taunted her for performing in a school production. He hated seeing his little daughter upset, so Lawrence sat her down and gave her a fatherly chat. He told her that she could achieve anything in life just as long as she wanted it enough. All she needed was total self-belief and never to let anyone cast a shadow of doubt over that belief. Lawrence had always lived life that way. He was his own man and had never cared what anyone thought about him. In Geri, he saw the same zest for life which had driven him, so he encouraged her to pursue her dreams and taught her to ignore the doubters. Throughout her teenage years, Lawrence was there for her and his guiding influence would underpin the raw determination Geri needed to achieve success.

Although Geri had her dad to support her emotional fears, there was little he could do to help with her physical insecurities, which became more serious in her teens. She was developing far later than her friends and while they were proudly showing off their curves, she was flat-chested, short and looked far younger than her age. It led to teasing and worries about boys. Geri remembered, 'I looked six when I was twelve. I remember slow-dancing with this guy and he went to put his hands up my top and there wasn't anything there. I was really embarrassed because I didn't even wear a bra.'

When a crowd of friends went to see Madonna's new film *Desperately Seeking Susan,* Geri was the only one who had trouble getting in. She was twelve and the film was a PG certificate for thirteen- to fifteen-year-olds. She had plastered her face with make-up and padded out her chest, but was still questioned about her age. It was embarrassing and Geri hated it, but the woman at the ticket office let her in anyway, probably because she felt sorry for her. The teasing about her size helped sharpen Geri's quick wit and she learned how to cut the most insulting bully dead with her barbed tongue.

When she turned sixteen, she finally blossomed and put the other girls to shame with her womanly figure. The new curves also heralded a dramatic change in Geri's character. She became more confident and developed a voracious appetite for life outside Watford and got heavily into the London dance scene. She loved the wild energy of the clubs and it opened a whole new world to her.

Geri left school with just one A-level, in English Literature, and took up a travel and tourism course at college. She enjoyed the freedom of college life because it allowed her to buzz around the

London clubs and go to raves, but her heart wasn't in the course. She didn't want to study the dull theory of world travel, she wanted to do it for real. She was still not sure what she wanted to do with her life; all she knew was that she wanted excitement and glamour, not an office job and suburban normality. But she needed a direction, and she knew that once she found that, she could make it happen.

Geri loved dancing and one night at the Astoria nightclub in London's Tottenham Court Road a talent scout spotted her potential. The scout told her about the BCM nightclub in Majorca which was crying out for sexy dancers like her. The idea appealed to her, so after leaving college, Geri headed for Magaluf, the island's party town, where the streets are filled with bars and all night discos.

The BCM is one of Magaluf's most popular clubs. To keep the atmosphere at fever pitch, scantily-clad girls are paid to dance on high podiums, or in cages suspended ten feet above the giant dancefloor. Geri wanted one of those jobs, so she approached the manager, Tony Palmer. He wasn't particularly impressed by her figure or looks. She wasn't a leggy blonde stunner which the club usually went for, but he liked her cheeky confidence and agreed to give her a week's trial. Tony remembered, 'She told me I wouldn't be disappointed and I wasn't. After one night, I realised that saucy style of hers was going to pull in the crowds. One day she would be dressed from head to toe in leather, the next she was in a giant red wig. She was really wild and flirtatious.'

Geri quickly became one of the most popular girls at the club and easily earnt her meagre £3-an-hour wages for dancing non-stop for several hours every night. She loved dressing in outrageous costumes and teasing the men in the crowds. She started on the podiums, but it wasn't long before she graduated to the cages, which were reserved for the more erotic dancers who were paid more money. Geri relished the power she wielded over the young men in the club. They were kept comfortably out of groping distance, so it was safe, and she loved to flirt. But, at the end of the day – albeit a sun-drenched one in Majorca – it was just a job to Geri.

Although she kept herself away from the sex-hungry punters, it didn't stop her from having some fun with the staff at BCM. One guy she liked was DJ Ricardo Terradillos, who later claimed in a newspaper that he was Geri's first lover. He revealed, 'I quickly noticed her writhing about on one of the high podiums. I wanted to be with her because she was such a tease and flirted with all the men. When I started to get to know her, she'd come over to me and tell me that I was sexy and she would touch my bum. She was very good at making you feel special. It was about a month before we had sex, but it was worth waiting for. As a DJ, I always had lots of girls, but Geri was special and that first night was very memorable. To me, Geri was a goddess and she always will be.'

Geri enjoyed the holiday atmosphere of Magaluf and her relationship with Ricardo. She hung out with a group of other British workers, but, while they partied wildly every night, Geri held back a little. She was on a different agenda and her mind was constantly thinking about her future. When the working crowd chatted, Geri would always tell them that she would be famous one day. It became a bit of a joke and the common reaction was, 'Oh, yeah, Geri, in your dreams!' They looked at her as just another club dancer with no special talent who was deluding herself. The other girls humoured her, but their mocking laughter didn't bother Geri – she had convinced herself it was going to happen. One girl who knew Geri in Magaluf said, 'She worked very hard at her dancing and you could tell the club was just a stepping stone for her. She was certain she was going to be a star. We found her really funny because she kept going on about being famous one day, but now we realise she has had the last laugh.'

Despite Geri's inner certainty that she was destined to make it, she was still stumped for the way to make her name. Dancing was all she seemed to know and that wasn't going to make her famous. But then she heard about Sebastian Amengual, a Spanish photographer, who had come to the club looking for a girl to pose for a magazine cover. Modelling – now that was a job she could do, Geri thought.

Rejection followed almost instantly when Sebastian chose Kelly Smith, another dancer and one of Geri's friends. But Geri wasn't dispirited. In fact, rejection created more of a challenge and, when she wanted something, she knew how to get it. She put her cheeky flirtatious charm into overdrive and cajoled the photographer until he agreed to take pictures of her, too. There was one slight drawback, he told her, she would have to pose naked. That wasn't a problem, Geri said, it would be part of the fun! Sebastian remembered, 'When I said I couldn't take her picture, Geri was determined to change my mind. She sidled up to me, gave me a cheeky smile and said, "Please do some photos of me as well."

'She was so small. I needed a tall, slender model, but she wouldn't take no for an answer. She was so persistent. She told me she wanted to be famous and she would try anything to help her move on. She begged me to take the photos. She kept on at me until I agreed. I warned her that she would have to model topless, but she said she didn't care.'

Sebastian took Geri to a disused factory site near the capital Palma for the future Spice Girl's first of many topless and nude photo sessions. He was amazed by her natural confidence in front of the camera. Sebastian said, 'I had to catch my breath, she looked so fantastic and had a wonderful body. I have never seen a body like it. I was fighting to control myself. She was so sexy. I just thought, "Oh my God." I am used to photographing naked girls, but she was special.'

In that first session, she posed for a standard series of glamour shots in just hold-up fishnet stockings and high shoes and then simply naked in the shoes. Her long brown hair hung down in ringlets and in a couple of poses she wore just sun-glasses and stood seductively on an iron staircase. In some photos she bore an uncanny resemblance to Madonna when she had posed topless years before she became famous. As with Madonna, Geri's topless career would come back to haunt her later, but she would have no regrets. Geri said, 'I never considered myself pretty enough to go in front of a camera. I never really felt exploited at the time. It was fine, I saw it for what it was.'

Geri went on to do more than twenty glamour sessions over the next few years and posed for Sebastian several more times around Majorca. In a later shoot, when her hair was short and dyed jet black, he took her to a secluded bay to pose against the rocks. They didn't know that a group of soldiers were enjoying the private show through binoculars. When they finally realised, they could have packed up and moved on, but Geri wasn't bothered – the more attention the better.

Such was Geri's ambition to get on that she didn't fall into the trap of remaining in the holiday resort worker clique, and she did just one season in Majorca before coming home with renewed determination to find fame. She was only nineteen, but as far as she was concerned, time was pushing on and she was in a hurry to make it. Not long after returning from Majorca, she began a rigorous fitness regime to get her body into peak shape. She was mentally ready for her assault on fame, but she knew she had to be physically perfect to seize any chance that came her way. The competition out there was tough and she felt her limited professional expertise meant she had to get the very best out of what she had. She showed her iron will when she hired fitness instructor Ray

McKenna as her private trainer. He gave her a daily workout which began at 6.45 am with a forty-five-minute run, followed by body toning and weights at the flat Geri was renting. Ray said, 'I couldn't believe how determined she was. She would say to me, "I'm going to be famous and I want my body to be perfect." It was already pretty good. Her bum was fantastic, but she was worried about her stomach and upper arms.

'It would still be dark when we went running and it was cold and rainy, but she would never complain. She was more dedicated than anyone I know. She was so fit and had amazing stamina. After the run she still had the energy for a full work-out. She could do a hundred sit-ups without a problem. One New Year's Eve she had stayed in and she rang me the next day morning at 9 am to do a workout. That was how determined she was.'

Geri continued with glamour modelling, hoping it could pave the way to stardom, or at least provide the big break she needed so badly. She posed for many more sessions with various photographers around London. One series was at a disused warehouse in London for John Smetherland who revealed, 'Geri seemed well at ease with every position I asked her to take. I still remember the shoot well because she was one of the most assertive models I've come across. She even ended up giving me some new ideas on how to photograph beautiful women.'

In another session, Geri posed for topless shots with a strategically placed feather boa, but her burgeoning topless career ruffled a few feathers with certain people. Her mum didn't like it and some of Geri's friends felt it was a bit tacky, but Lawrence Halliwell backed his daughter. He thought the pictures were wonderful and agreed they might well open the door to something better.

Lawrence emerged as Geri's greatest supporter during this frustrating and sometimes desperate period. Now approaching seventy, his health was deteriorating, yet Lawrence always found the time and energy to give unwavering support to his daughter. Most people sniggered behind Geri's back when she went on about her quest for fame, but her dad never doubted her. He listened to her dreams and bolstered her resolve if ever it waned. In turn, Geri brought love and excitement into his life. Although very demanding, her optimism and her boundless enthusiasm were a constant joy. Lawrence loved being with Geri and he devoted much of what would tragically prove to be his last years helping her find the success she dreamed of.

Geri started going to dance auditions and screen tests for television work all over London and her dad became her self-appointed chauffeur making sure she got wherever she needed to be on time. She was relatively new to that circuit and it must have come as a shock to be up against girls who had trained at drama schools and dance colleges for years. Month after month, she slogged from one audition to the next. One break was as an extra in a Pink Floyd video where she met a young man called David Apstein, who also had a few days work on the shoot. They got on well and began a brief fling. David, who was a few years younger than Geri, witnessed how determined she was to succeed. He revealed later, 'In the short time I was with Geri, it was a real eye-opener for me because I was quite inexperienced. It seemed just like a holiday fling because it happened so quickly. There were no love letters, flowers or meals, just sex. I knew she'd make it big one day. She was definitely a career girl who thought more of her future than she did of me.'

Her career was so important that there seemed little time in Geri's life for a steady relationship. She told David that she'd not had sex for nearly a year before they met. Despite being so attractive and sexy, it would appear Geri was happier flirting than getting too involved. This was certainly true when she worked as an aerobics instructor to earn money while she was waiting for stardom. Liam

Fitzgerald, the owner of the gym where she worked, said, 'Geri was a publicity machine for my gym. She always wore a G-string leotard over a tight T-shirt. Men just came to watch her. When she jumped up and down they steamed up the glass panel wall. I removed it in the end because we had to clean it so much. Everyone fancied her, but she was brilliant at verbal judo and could put men down without being cruel. No one dared ask her out.'

Geri did all kinds of jobs during this period. She worked in bars, did cleaning and sold cheap imitation watches. She did anything to get by, but all the time her mind was constantly ticking over trying to focus on the avenue which would lead to the fame she craved. She started to think about a career in pop music. Although she couldn't play an instrument and had limited singing experience, the idea appealed to her. The music industry was awash with overnight stars and it seemed the fastest route to fame. After all, wasn't the queen of wannabees, Madonna, a perfect example of what was possible? So, Geri spent £300 recording a demo tape of herself singing some cover versions.

But, before she had fully invented herself as a pop star, Geri got a break in television. The good news was that she would be the glamorous hostess responsible for exhibiting prizes on *The Price Is Right* gameshow, which had been a hit on British television. The bad news was that Geri's job was on the Turkish version of the show. But she wasn't bothered. Compared to dancing in a cage above a heaving dance floor in Majorca, it was a fantastic break and she happily flew to Istanbul to record the shows. She threw herself into the work with her usual exuberance, showing off the prizes while dressed to the nines in evening wear. As far as she was concerned, it was better to have TV experience in Turkey than none at all at home. It was another valuable stepping stone in the right direction.

Back in Britain, she continued plugging away trying to break into television, whilst still keeping her eye on pop music. She started making some good contacts and was proving to be a master at networking. Finally, she landed a job at the cable station L!ve TV presenting a new show called *Fashion Police*. The off-beat show involved Geri racing around London in a taxi with a film crew and jumping out to stop people in the street she considered to be badly dressed. She would yell, 'We're the fashion police and you're nicked!' The idea was to poke fun at the fashion victims of the capital. It seemed a good enough idea on paper but in practice it didn't work and was quickly scrapped. It may have been disappointing for Geri but all was not lost because the bosses at L!ve thought she was perfect for television and promised to find her another presenting job.

As Geri celebrated her twenty-first birthday in August 1993, it seemed she was at last finding some direction. Positive things were starting to happen and, although she had a long way to go, she felt she was getting somewhere. But three months later, in November, her world was devastated when her dad died suddenly. Lawrence Halliwell was seventy-one and his health had been deteriorating throughout that year. All his children were heartbroken by his death, but Geri took it hardest of all. Her dad had always backed her and it seemed so cruel he should be taken away just when she was on the threshold of a breakthrough. For Geri, there would always be a deep, enduring sadness that her father would never see her reach such incredible heights of success with the Spice Girls.

It took Geri several painful months to come to terms with losing her father. There were countless tears, but as the long bleak winter gave way to the spring of 1994, she refocused her ambitions with renewed vigour. Maybe the brutal suddenness of his death made her even more determined to make something of her life. Fate then presented the opportunity to join a new pop group and Geri knew she must seize that chance.

That cheeky, cajoling phone conversation with Chris Herbert was straight out of the Lawrence Halliwell school of chancing your arm. His spirit lived on in his youngest child and he would have been proud.

— 5 —

TANTRUMS AND TEARS

The second and final audition took place on 17 May at NOMIS and Geri made her mark right from the beginning. The same team of judges, plus Chic, were there to spend a day with the ten girls and choose a final five. Very little was known about Geri, so one of the men asked how old she was. Geri flashed a devilish grin and replied, 'I'll be as old as you want me to be. I'll be ten with big boobs if you want!' She was cheeky like that throughout the day and her wit and personality shone through. She quickly sussed out that Chic was one of the key people within the decision-making group. She called him 'Chicky Baby' and proceeded to win him over with her charm.

The ten girls spent the day doing various dance routines, harmonies and solo singing *a cappella*. They were put into two groups initially and told to choreograph a full routine to an Eternal song. The judges wanted to see how the girls blended together in a work situation and to discover who had the strongest personalities. All the time, the judges were looking for each girl's best qualities and paid particular attention to which ones got on well together.

Mel B had good choreography ideas and Mel C had a strong voice, and both were gutsy girls with attitude. Victoria Adams and Michelle Stephenson added a touch of glamour. Geri was still the wild card but her character stole the show and the three men felt her personality and drive would rub off on the other four girls they liked.

The final choices were made a short time after that day and the five girls were invited down for a trial week of rehearsals to see if the group was workable. They were put up in a guest house near Woking in Surrey, and taken to Trinity Studios, a complex of rehearsal and recording facilities in Knaphill, a small village three miles outside Woking. Ian Lee, the artistic director at Trinity, had been helping out the Herberts with equipment since the first audition. He had seen all the video footage and was familiar with the project. He remembers the first time he met the girls well. He said, 'They were all shy and nervous, just like most people are on the first day of a new job, that is except Geri. She tottered in on her platform shoes, full of confidence, and introduced herself. She said "Hi, I'm Geri. Who are you? Oooh, this is going to be fun, isn't it?" She seemed to be loving it already.'

The first song the girls worked on was called 'Take Me Away' by Erwin Keiles and John Thirkell, two songwriters Bob and Chris had known for years. After five days of exhausting rehearsals, the girls had to perform a mini gig for the management team, including Chic, and various other people at the studios. They had made good progress and everyone was impressed. A plan was then laid out for how the group would be developed and the girls were asked if they wanted to go for it. The answer was a resounding Yes.

The hard slog to stardom began in the first week of June 1994. Trinity Studios became the girls' second home and it was here that the embryonic pop group was moulded and trained. But the girls' main home was a three-bedroom, 1970s semi-detached house at 58 Boyn Hill Road, just outside Maidenhead town centre and a twenty-five-minute drive from Trinity. Chic paid for a shower room to be installed in the downstairs cloakroom because it would have been impossible for five girls to cope with one bathroom.

The practical work for pop fame may have been done at Trinity, but the gang spirit of attitude and Girl Power which would define the Spice Girls simmered in that ramshackle house until it was ready to explode and seize control.

As the work started, the girls were given a strict work schedule. Bob and Chris sorted out four more songs with completed backing tracks from the Keiles/Thirkell catalogue and the girls were told to work out their own dance routines to those songs. There were no choreographers or stylists brought in at the beginning as was standard with most manufactured groups. Chris wanted them to develop naturally and let their own style breathe, rather than let it be smothered by professional ideas. He wanted the group to have genuine foundations and character, which would greatly increase its chances of survival.

One of the first things a new band needs is a name. Everyone joked about becoming Take This and various other silly girl variations of boy band names, then Chris came up with Touch. No one particularly liked it, and then again, no one hated it. Touch was catchy and had a certain sexiness, so they decided to keep it as a working name.

There was very little flippancy from any of the girls in those early days. In fact, they were the model of politeness, like pupils at a new school finding their feet, sticking to the rules for fear of being told off. The staff at the studios never even heard them swear. They were so demure that onlookers would feel embarrassed as Chic illustrated his advice with colourful four-letter words. Ian Lee saw those early rehearsals. He said, 'Chic was always swearing and he didn't care that they were young girls. God knows what they must have thought. The girls were very conscientious right from the beginning. They arrived for work at about 9.30–10am and stayed through until about 4–5pm, with a few coffee breaks and a lunch break. In those first few weeks, they were still getting to know each other, so they were quiet, as if they were sizing each other up.

'The dance routines were pretty bad, but they slowly came together and you could see that Mel B was the one with the ideas. The weak link with the dancing was definitely Geri. They would do a routine but it would keep breaking down because Geri got the steps wrong. She would say, "Hang on, I've lost it, let's do that again," and they would all have to start from scratch. But you would often see Geri in the studio on her own practising the steps while the others were having a coffee break. Then you would hear her shout out, "I've got it! I've got it!" She was always very enthusiastic.'

Although Geri had difficulty with some dance routines, it was soon obvious that *all* the girls needed vocal tuning. They could sing, but lacked professional technique, so the management decided they needed a vocal coach. Erwin Keiles suggested Pepi Lemer, whom he knew well. Pepi is one of the top singing teachers in the music business and, after twelve years of teaching, has coached some top recording artists. Even established stars hire her to fine-tune their already exquisite voices. At the other end of the scale, Pepi can also turn raw beginners into accomplished singers. She was invited to Trinity where the girls sang 'Take Me Away' for her.

'My immediate reaction was that there was a lot of work needed here,' said Pepi. 'I made a whole load of notes and then went outside with Chic, Bob and Chris. I told them the girls looked good and had potential, but that it would take a lot of time to get them right. I asked how long they would give me and then we started talking about money and lessons. We finally agreed on two sessions a week for four or five hours each with an initial period of three months.'

And so it was handed to Pepi to turn the girls into quality singers. It would prove to be an exhausting challenge and an adventure, but nothing prepared Pepi for the confrontation in the first lesson. She took each girl through a series of scales and exercises to determine their vocal ranges, making notes as she went along. She soon realised the overall job would be harder than she had originally thought. All the girls would need comprehensive individual coaching if they were to stand any chance of singing in harmony. During a break, Pepi made the mistake of leaving her notepad on view. She recalled, 'I came back in the room and Geri was on her own by the window. She turned round to look at me and her faced was flushed and full of anger. She was really unhappy and rounded on me and said, "You think I'm out of tune."

'She had read my notes while I was out and was really upset. Tears were filling her eyes, but she was trying to fight them back. She said, "Working together is going to be really difficult now this has happened." The other girls could hear what she was saying. I was quite taken aback because she was so angry. She clearly had a very strong defensive mechanism which clicked in when she felt threatened.

'I remember thinking, I don't need this, so I took her to the other side of the studio and sat her down on a chair and gave it to her straight. I said, "There is no place for sensitivity in this business. If you are going to cry and take it personally when I say things are wrong, then you may as well go now, because we won't be able to work together and you will not survive in showbusiness. I will make copious notes about your ability, but I'm here to help you. You should rejoice in that fact and take everything I tell you positively; it will make you better. Yes, you are out of tune, you won't be forever, but only if you take notice of me." She listened to me carefully and didn't answer back or fight me. Geri is very clued in and bright and she knew I was talking sense. She was very cool about it. She looked at me and said, "OK," and I said, "Right, let's forget about it and start again."

'From then on, Geri and I didn't have any more problems and I really came to respect her. She responded so well to everything I told her. Often during breaks, I would see her in a corner practising her diaphragm breathing or doing various vocal exercises, while the others were having a chat. I really admired her determination. I know Chic liked her, too, because one day later I said to him something like, "What are we going to do with her," and he said, "We'll have to work with what we've got because she's got tremendous personality and stage presence. I don't want to lose her."'

There was no way they would lose Geri. Quite the reverse would happen.

The girls settled into a routine. Every morning they would start with a warm-up period of physical stretches to keep them in shape for dance routines and then they would do their vocal exercises. Ian Lee set up five microphones and a PA system which played the backing tracks to the five songs they had to work on. They sweated for hours on end, perfecting their act and getting the choreography for each number as tight as possible.

There were many tense moments in those first few weeks. It was impossible to maintain any creativity and flow of ideas without disagreements and the rows soon started. There were two extremes of personalities in the group: Mel C, Michelle and Victoria, who were relatively quiet and bottled things up to avoid confrontations; and Geri and Mel B, the two dominant girls, who would say exactly what they thought and have an argument. Tempers became so frayed with everyone living and working together that they all agreed to make a pact which would help maintain their sanity: if anyone wasn't happy about something or someone, they had to get it out in the open so it could be discussed. Nothing was allowed to go unsaid. It was a very mature and foresighted solution which worked well and created a lasting bond between the girls.

There were still blazing rows, but nothing festered. Mel B and Geri clashed continually and were very wary of each other in the beginning. Neither liked to take criticism without fighting back. Mel B was the strongest dancer and the one with the choreography skills, but Geri had her ideas too and wanted them used. They were often locked on a collision course, but neither would change direction or put the brake on, so they would crash head on into a blazing row. The fall-out echoed through Trinity on a daily basis. A backing tape would suddenly stop in mid-song and be replaced with raised voices; the volume would escalate into shouting and would generally culminate with the loud slam of a door as one or more of the girls stormed out in fury. The steam soon dispersed, though, and the music would start up. The atmosphere would be healthier for the row and the work, whether it be choreography or singing, benefited from the clash of ideas. A vibrant sense of teamwork developed out of those differences. Geri and Mel B would always remain the dominant figures who took control of the group and, slowly, they became great friends.

The genuine bonding between the girls was exactly what the management wanted. That was how they would develop into a real group with foundations, not a one-dimensional pre-fabricated shell. But it exposed one major flaw in the design: Michelle.

After five or so weeks, as the rehearsal period moved into August, it was clear there was a gulf between Michelle and the other four girls, and everyone was starting to notice it. The girls knew she wasn't fitting in, the management suspected it, and even the guys around the studio sensed something wasn't working. Michelle was progressing technically, but she always appeared to be the odd one out. At lunch times, the girls normally nipped out to the local Sainsbury's to buy a sandwich, but Michelle would stay on her own at the studio or lie in the sun outside. Ian Lee spotted the gap. He said, 'The girls started to gel as a gang, but it was clear Michelle wasn't part of that gang. There was no antagonism and it wasn't personal, it was just that she was a different animal to the others. They were street-wise, a bit naughty and bubbly, and were having a laugh in the group. Michelle was a more stable, methodical and academic type, who saw it as more of a job. I suppose you could say she lacked attitude.'

Maybe Michelle's heart wasn't totally in the group which accounted for her not being part of the gang mentality. It also emerged that she was coping with a shattering family trauma; her mother, Penny, had breast cancer. Finally, Michelle left the group to look after her mum and to re-focus on her academic career.

As Touch coped with losing Michelle, another problem was bubbling under the surface. Victoria had been acting slightly mischievously because she was still in the other group, Persuasion. Basically, she had been leading two lives.

Who knows what was going on in her head that summer, but it must have been a nightmare for her. She had experienced many disappointments in her fledgling showbusiness career and she didn't want any more, so when she was faced with two chances of stardom, she had grabbed them both. Since the Dance Works audition, she had been secretly riding both horses, desperately holding on to both, trying to suss out which was the winner. But now she had to make a decision.

Work with Persuasion had intensified in August because the group had been rehearsing hard for a showcase concert for record industry executives to be held on 28 August at the Discotheque Royal in Uxbridge. It would be the big night that would launch the band and, hopefully, secure a record deal. The pressure built up in Victoria.

Touch had begun with few promises but now the girls had been together for a while, she could sense something special was developing between them. She knew she had to stick with them and finally decided to make that dreaded phonecall to Pesuasion's manager Steve Andrews – just twelve days before the concert. He said, 'It was our big chance to become famous. Victoria kept checking that she was doing everything right – she was really nervous because she was singing the lead in a ballad. I brought in a solicitor and was set to get everyone on a contract to show that we meant business. Our dreams really started to take shape. It had taken a lot of work, but we were ready. Then she rang and said she had to leave for her other band. I remember it like it was yesterday. She knew damn well we couldn't replace her before the launch. I was so angry I couldn't speak. I kept asking her how she could do it to all of us and she kept apologising. We were all devastated when she quit – we couldn't believe what she had done to us. It felt like we had been kicked in the teeth.'

Persuasion pulled up lame and out of the pop fame stakes, while Touch galloped on. There was a long way left to run and many tricky fences to clear, but Victoria had backed the winner.

The four girls had a summer break while the Herberts were left to find a replacement for Michelle. They considered girls who had made the short-list at NOMIS, but soon realised they needed a new face. They asked Pepi if she knew of anyone suitable and she immediately thought of a girl she had been teaching privately – Abigail Kis.

Abigail was very interested and auditioned well. She clearly had the look and talent to fill the gap left by Michelle, but Chic was on his finest, bluntest form that day. Abigail had brought her boyfriend to the audition, but Chic didn't like his girls to have boyfriends; he saw them as a threat to his investment. He decided to put her to the test and said she would have to be single to get the job. The boyfriend protested and Chic said coarsely, 'How are you going to feel when thousands of blokes are ogling your bird in a short skirt?'

It was the flipside to an encouraging recruitment talk and it did the trick: it put Abigail right off and she later called to politely tell Pepi it wasn't for her. It was a decision she would live to regret and, somewhat predictably, the boyfriend didn't last.

Several other girls were auditioned, but then Pepi remembered a girl she had taught at Barnet Technical College. She was a kind natured, pretty girl with a sweet voice. Her name was Emma Bunton.

– 6 –

AND BABY
MAKES FIVE

EMMA'S STORY

It proved hard to trace Emma because she had already left college and Pepi didn't have her home number. The college lecturer Pepi contacted took some time in coming back to her, but finally found the number. Emma was out when Pepi called, so Pepi spoke to her mum, Pauline, who vaguely remembered her daughter's singing teacher. Pepi was low-key about the idea. 'I'm not sure if Emma would be interested,' she said, 'but I'm working with this group. They're not much at the moment, but they have some people behind them who are very serious and are spending a lot of money getting them right. It probably won't lead anywhere, but do you think it's one for Emma?'

A few hours later, Emma called. She was excited and, yes, she was very interested.

Although Emma had passed her drama course at Barnet Tech, she had no work lined up before that fateful call from Pepi. It wasn't yet time to panic about her future, but Emma was in a position to expect slightly more of her career. She was only eighteen, but she had already enjoyed thirteen successful years in the business and was eager to move on to greater things.

Emma Lee Bunton was born on 21 January 1976 and brought up in Finchley, North London, with her brother, Paul, who is five years younger. Emma's natural desire for the spotlight began in her toddler years. When she was eighteen months old, she charmed the locals celebrating the Queen's Silver Jubilee in 1977 when she was dressed as a pearly queen in a sequinned outfit. With her blonde hair, angelic smile and sweet nature, she was like a doll who brought admiring comments from every adult.

When she was three, Emma won a holiday camp beauty contest and posed happily on a makeshift throne in a tiny crown and regal cloak. She sparkled in front of the camera and the limelight attracted her like a magnet. Such was Emma's love of being on show, that when she was five, Pauline Bunton took her for a casting at a child modelling agency where she was quickly signed up by an agent. Work flooded in immediately and signalled the start of Emma's colourful career as a child model. She was constantly on the move for castings and photo sessions. Her agent, Gill Peters, said, 'Emma was a hit. She never stopped working and had that special something that we were looking for. She had a twinkle in her eye and she loved the camera.'

Emma did all kinds of work. She posed in a knitting pattern advert for a mail order catalogue and then appeared in a Mothercare brochure. When she was six she appeared in a boy meets girl photo, pretending to share a glass of red wine, which was really Ribena, with a boyfriend.

As well as having precocious confidence in front of the lens, Emma was also eager to learn how to sing and dance, so her mum enrolled her at the Kay Dance school near her home for ballet and tap lessons. Her first stage part was as a moonbeam and then as a tap-dancing bear cub. One of her teachers in those days was Sheryle

Adrian, who recalled, 'Emma was a skinny little stick. I will never forget how she fitted in, even with children two years older, and I remember when she picked up a particularly complicated routine right away. She was extremely good at everything, so I knew she would go far. She could have pursued ballet full-time, but she wanted a more rounded training.'

Not everyone was thrilled by such a pressurised career for a little girl and some felt Emma was missing out on a normal childhood in pursuit of fame. Certainly her grandmother, Theresa Bunton, felt uneasy. She said, 'Emma was always pushed as a child and was being rushed from one audition to the next. She was never outside playing with other kids or with her dollies. As soon as I came in the room she would say, "Nanny, watch me tap dance, watch my ballet." Of course, I was proud of everything she did, but in some ways she didn't have a childhood. Even in our holiday snaps, Emma was always posing, constantly playing the little model. We all said Emma would be someone special. She was a little dolly, the prettiest thing you have ever seen.'

Whatever childhood joys Emma was missing, she was more than replacing them with the experience and fun that came with modelling. She would travel all round London and occasionally abroad to sunny locations and she was earning fantastic money for a child. In the early days, she earnt £20 an hour, which was put away in an account to help her later. One of the biggest benefits of the career was the special relationship it created between Emma and her mum who travelled everywhere with her daughter to make sure she was happy and well looked after. They became like best friends, and that bond would help Emma cope with the pressure once she found international fame.

An early sign of Emma's pop star pretensions came when she was nine. Madonna mania was just starting to sweep Britain following her hit 'Like A Virgin' and Emma loved her as much as anyone. For her ninth birthday in 1985, she had a party with a Madonna theme. At school, Emma would also organise impromptu pop groups in the playground – naturally, with her as the lead singer – and at home she would spend hours in her bedroom pretending to record her own radio show.

Emma was already a seasoned professional model by the age of ten. She had so much experience that she would often look after the younger children if ever they got upset during a tiring photo shoot. One of her most prestigious jobs came when she modelled for Harrods where she appeared on a catwalk in swimsuits and colourful outfits with matching accessories such as red heart-shaped sunglasses. She was also the face on boxes of Persil washing powder and the girl who brushed her teeth with pink Mentadent toothpaste. She was also the Milky Bar Kid's girlfriend in a TV commercial, while in Switzerland she was known as the little girl who ate fresh strawberries.

With such an unusual childhood, it was inevitable that Emma wouldn't stay in mainstream education, so she joined the Sylvia Young Drama School, in North London, a highly respected stage school for child performers. Emma was in her element there. All the other girls were outrageous extroverts like herself and she joined a class of young wannabees, many of whom would find fame, although on a far more modest scale than her. In her class was Daniella Westbrook, who would star in the BBC soap *EastEnders*, Dani Behr who would become a TV presenter, and Samantha Janus, a stage and TV actress of the future. Another classmate was Denise Van Outen, the current presenter of Channel 4's *The Big Breakfast*. Together they were a wild bunch who enjoyed flirting with boys and generally causing mischief. Denise remembered, 'Me and Emma were the two blondes at school. That made us quite popular with the boys, so

**R.U. 18-23 WITH THE ABILITY
TO SING/DANCE
R.U. STREETWISE, OUTGOING,
AMBITIOUS & DEDICATED**

HEART MANAGEMENT LTD
are a widely successful
Music Industry Management Consortium
currently forming a choreographed, Singing/Dancing,
all Female Pop Act for a Record Recording Deal.
OPEN AUDITION
DANCE WORKS, 16 Balderton Street,
FRIDAY 4TH MARCH
11.00am - 5.30pm
PLEASE BRING SHEET MUSIC
OR BACKING CASSETTE

Heart Management Ltd

The original advert in *The Stage* on 24 February 1994
to announce the open audition

Ginger Spice
Geri Halliwell
strikes a pose
for the
camera

Posh Spice Victoria
Adams with her
trademark scowl

Scary Spice Melanie Brown screams for Girl Power

Baby Spice Emma Bunton looks sweet in her baby-doll outfit

Sporty Spice Melanie Chisholm gives a hearty karate kick

The girls during one of their first photo sessions before their launch

Geri lets a photographer
know what she thinks as he
catches her out shopping

The Spice Girls on the
threshold of fame soon
after 'Wannabe' went
to No. 1 in July 1996

The gang enjoys a wild
night at a television
awards ceremony

Emma sobbed when a
paparazzi photographer
took this picture of her
with mum Pauline on
holiday in Barbados

Sporty Mel C looks lean and fit for a night out at the trendy Metropolitan Bar

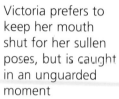

Victoria prefers to keep her mouth shut for her sullen poses, but is caught in an unguarded moment

The girls get ready to rock at the
Capital Radio Roadshow in July 1996

Victoria just about manages a festive smile as the girls prepare to switch on the Oxford Street Christmas lights

In contrast, Geri gets into the spirit and shows Girl Power by lifting a fan in Oxford Street

Patriotic Geri caused a stir at the Brit Awards with this outrageous Union Jack micro-dress

Victoria chats on her mobile phone just after parking her new sports car, one of the first things she bought once the Spice Girls' money finally flowed in

The girls accept
one of their Brit
Awards

Geri shows off her
prized jewels and
laughed later,
'Everyone has seen
them before!'

The girls raised a fortune for Comic Relief by donating proceeds from the 'Mama'/'Who Do You Think You Are?' single

Emma's enchanting smile gave her a successful career as a child model

The girls celebrate the launch of the album *Spice*

Mel B raises her trophy after being named Spectacle Wearer of the Year

Mel B prowls the stage in a
leopard catsuit at the Brits

The Spice Girls use Girl Power to switch on Channel 5

Geri arrives in outrageous style for the Prince's Trust concert

The Spice Girls give their first live performance
in Britain at the Prince's Trust concert

Shortly after ambushing Prince Charles the girls joined the
official line-up with the other stars at the Prince's Trust concert

The girls arrived Hollywood-style for the
Cannes Film Festival in May 1997

The girls left photographers all at sea by
jumping aboard this boat at Cannes

we'd snog them, then pass them around. We'd meet in the toilets at breaktime and talk about the boys we'd kissed – quite often you'd find you'd been kissing the same ones. Girls outnumbered boys at our school, so it was share and share alike. At lunchtimes we would put loads of make-up on in the toilets, roll our skirts up to make them shorter, then jump on the canteen tables to do songs from *Fame*. But as soon as the head caught up with us, the make-up came off, the skirts went back down and we were ordered down off the tables. Emma was a great singer and a lovely person. She was never bitchy and everyone liked her. Even then she always wore her hair in bunches.'

In between the crazy behaviour at Sylvia Young, Emma learnt all aspects of performing, from acting to singing and dancing. She played a number of roles in school productions and went up for many theatrical castings. One of the biggest auditions she had as a teenager was for the part of Bianca, a newly scripted young tearaway in *EastEnders*. The casting director liked Emma and put her on the final short-list of six, but she wasn't chosen. It was a near miss at fame because Bianca went on to be one of the soap's most popular young characters and to secure stardom for Patsy Palmer. Later, Emma did secure a walk-on part in *EastEnders* as a member of a gang which mugged one of Albert Square's pensioners. It was a good break but the role didn't befit her sweet character, which upset her grandmother who commented, 'Couldn't you have a landed a nicer role?'

Although some of Emma's drama school fees were paid for out of her earnings over the previous years, it wasn't enough to cover everything and the Buntons struggled to keep up. Her dad Trevor, a milkman, worked extra rounds and took a second job at night as a mini-cab driver to afford the fees. But the strain on the family finances became too great and Emma had to leave Sylvia Young to go back to an ordinary secondary school. It was a difficult time for

Emma and she found it hard to adjust, but, thankfully, she had shown so much potential that it wasn't long before she was offered a scholarship at Sylvia Young and was able to return.

Emma was sixteen when she met her first serious boyfriend. Out of the small group of boys at stage school, Carlton Morgan was one of the better-looking ones and he was instantly besotted by her. He revealed, 'Emma stood out because she was so pretty. She was the first girl who made me think, Yes, I've got to have her. I didn't want to steam in and ruin my chances, so I put the word out that I was interested. A few days later she came up to me and said, "I hear you like me. What are you going to do about it! Why don't you walk me home." I went with her to the station and I've never walked so slowly. Then I kissed her and things went from there.'

The relationship quickly grew serious. They made sure they were together throughout breaktimes and as much as possible after school. When they were apart, they would spend hours talking on the phone and romantic Carlton would sing Michael Jackson's 'I Just Can't Stop Loving You' to her down the line. During their time together, Emma was trying to write songs of her own and whenever she wrote a love ballad, she would sing it to Carlton. They went out together for six months before they made love for the first time – to the sounds of Whitney Houston's 'Greatest Love of All'. Carlton said, 'It was very special and a time I'll never forget. Emma was nervous, not knowing what to do, but she seemed to enjoy herself. Every time I hear that song I smile to myself. We both knew this was more than a teenage romance. We felt deeply for each other and talked about the day we'd get married and start a family. We were pretty wild, but we were in love and did whatever we could to be together.' Emma later spoke of her first sexual experience and revealed, 'It didn't all run smoothly, but it was beautiful. I stayed with the boy for a year and it got better and better each time.'

The relationship ended when Carlton's parents split up and he had to leave school to help look after his younger brother and sister. It was a traumatic time for Carlton, but Emma could sympathise because her parents had also separated when she was younger. She had to live with her grandparents round the corner from her house in Finchley while her mum and dad sorted out the break, which ultimately ended in divorce. It was an upsetting time, but Emma's passion for performing helped side-track her mind. Once the separation was finalised, Emma and her brother moved in with their mum. Pauline later worked as a karate teacher running classes locally and she helped coach Emma to blue-belt standard.

Emma left Sylvia Young when she was sixteen and began a two-year drama course at Barnet Technical College where she appeared in many musical productions and plays. There she met Pepi Lemer who helped develop her sweet voice and improved her so much that often Emma's solo spots in productions stole the show.

While at Barnet, she continued going up for castings and managed to land many parts in big television commercials. One of her high profile jobs was in a Halifax building society advert in which she was a bridesmaid on the top tier of a wedding cake made of people. But the competition is fierce in showbusiness and, despite so many years of experience and some of the best training, Emma found it hard to secure a big acting break.

In the final term at Barnet, she applied for university places, only to be rejected. She was very disappointed and left college to an uncertain future and in the two months that followed she had no success. Only the odd cheque through the post for TV commercial repeat fees served as a reminder of her showbusiness career. But Emma is a strong believer in fate and all the time she believed deep down that something would turn up. Then the phone call from Pepi came.

'I was very realistic when I spoke to Emma,' Pepi recalled. 'She said she wasn't doing much and was happy to have a go at anything. I didn't want to get her hopes up because 90 per cent of auditions don't lead anywhere. But she wanted to do it and she said, "Thank you so much for thinking of me, Pepi." Emma is a really sweet, polite girl.'

Pepi sent Emma a tape of 'Take Me Away' and told her to learn it while she set up an audition. It was to be held at Erwin Keiles's house in West London where the third bedroom was converted into a recording studio. The house was hard to find, so Emma and her mum followed Pepi there in the car.

Emma sang well for Chris, Bob, Erwin and Chic, although her nerves made the high notes slightly shaky. They all liked her; well, all except Chic. He liked her voice and general look, but his main concern was far more cosmetic – he thought she was too fat! In particular, he thought her legs were too short. Chic liked legs and still secretly yearned to create a replica of the Three Degrees. Emma, a tiny, pale girl in blonde bunches, was about as far away from that image as you could get.

Pepi convinced Chic that most teenage girls carried a bit of puppy fat which disappeared as they matured. The Herberts remained adamant they didn't want an untouchable, statuesque model, and finally Chic agreed Emma was perfect. She was warned she would have to live with the other girls, which seemed a daunting prospect. She had always been a mummy's girl and dreaded the thought of leaving Pauline, but she knew she had to make the break and eagerly accepted the job.

In the first week, Emma found living at 58 Boyn Hill Road diffi-cult and would often sob down the phone to her mum. Geri found her crying in her bedroom one evening and immediately gave her a hug. All the girls seemed to want to mother Emma, so she quickly began to settle in after that first week. Emma isn't bitchy or openly competitive by nature, so she didn't antagonise or threaten the others, and her gentle character was a welcome antidote to the boisterous dominance of Geri and Mel B. They liked her instantly and one person who saw the five together in the first few weeks said it was like four aunties looking after their long-lost niece. The chasm that had been evident with Michelle vanished with Emma's arrival. The baby made the gang complete.

-7-

MAKING IT HAPPEN

Now Emma was aboard, the real graft began. A weekly rota was drawn up detailing which days to concentrate on songs, dance routines, or vocal training. It was a tough schedule, which meant they had to stick to a strict timetable, but the girls enthusiastically threw themselves into the work at Trinity Studios. There was no room for skiving, even if they had wanted to, because the management kept tabs on their input and monitored their progress on a more or less daily basis. Rather more ominously, their sugar daddy Chic kept a distant, but very keen eye on them. He would call the guys at the studios frequently to check what time the girls had started or clocked off. If ever he thought they were taking liberties, he made sure they knew he wasn't happy.

The girls signed on the dole to keep themselves going and claimed housing benefit to help with the accommodation expenses. They lived like students, going out when they could, but having to watch what they spent. They tried to save cash by taking homemade salads or sandwiches to work to avoid buying lunch every day from Sainsbury's or a coffee shop they liked in Knaphill village.

The daily singing and choreography routines they had begun with Michelle continued with Emma and she slotted in perfectly. She quickly caught up with the dance steps and was already at a good standard vocally, so she had little ground to make up. Most of the girls' work was directed at their reflection in a giant floor-to-ceiling mirror in the studio. They would stare incessantly into that mirror when they sang or danced, so they became acutely aware of their look and style.

They sang the five songs from the Keiles/Thirkell catalogue into their microphones over and over again until they were sick of them. One of the songs was aptly titled 'We're Gonna Make It Happen' and it became the girls' signature tune throughout those formative months.

The singing lessons with Pepi continued mostly at Trinity, but some days she took them at her home, or she visited the house in Boyn Hill Road. The lessons were long, exhausting and frustrating. Often they would spend hours in a semi-circle facing Pepi on the piano individually trying to sing certain notes. Pepi would play the note again and again until each girl got it right. At times they doubted whether they needed such perfection to make it in pop music, a world which was now dominated by computer technology to improve even the worst voices. But, ultimately, they would be grateful for Pepi's dedication and patience. They were pushed to breaking point and during one session at the house Mel B finally cracked. Pepi remembered, 'I was sitting on the keyboard upstairs in one of the bedrooms and was having a half-hour lesson with each girl. I was trying to get Mel B to sing a particular note. She was out of tune, but couldn't hear herself, so I made her try it again and again. It went on for ages, but she just couldn't get it right.

'She wasn't very open and had a real defence to her. She didn't take to teaching easily like some of the girls and would question what I was doing. We kept trying to get this note and in the end she started crying. Tears were rolling down her face. She was so upset she couldn't continue, so I said, "OK, let's give it a rest for today." She was pretty relieved to be let off. Later, I asked the other girls what the matter was and they told me she was having boyfriend problems.

'Mel came across as tough and had a tremendous strength of character, but she had her own vulnerability and was human just like the rest of the girls. They all cried at some point during the time I worked with them. There was always boyfriend trouble, or one was tired, the normal sorts of problems. But it wasn't surprising because the work was so intense. I was very worried about Emma at one point because she was so exhausted. She had no energy left, she was lethargic and would curl up looking as if she was cold the whole time. I thought about getting her to see a doctor, but she got stronger.

'The girls were under a lot of pressure and I really admired their determination. If they had been lazy and messed around, I would never have stuck with them; they wouldn't have seen me for dust because they had too much ground to cover, but I grew to like them a lot.

'They worked so hard, day after day, and their ambition kept me going, too. They were basically very nice girls and I wanted them to succeed because I could see how much they were putting in. I got on well with Geri after a while and she didn't get sensitive again, she went with everything I had to offer her. She drank it all in and I so admired her. She was more open with me and even became interested in my life. She was wonderful and you could tell she was bright and had a perspective on life. She acknowledged she had more work to do than the others, so she took it upon herself to do that and she caught the others up. Week by week, her voice got stronger and she eventually overtook them in the basic training because she put in more hours.'

Despite the tedious repetition of the five songs and the singing lessons, it wasn't all drudgery during this time and the girls still had plenty of laughs. As they evolved into a tight gang, they had in-jokes and in-words that only they knew, and people could easily feel uneasy with their overpowering presence. There were many laughs at the house and Pepi and Shelley D'Silva remember the mad atmosphere there. It was like a girlie version of *The Young Ones* and *Men Behaving Badly* television comedy shows rolled into one.

The house was sparsely furnished. It had a basic kitchen at the back of the house and cheap old furniture in the large lounge. A giant mirror was put up in that room for the girls to practice their choreography in the evenings. Upstairs, there were two big bedrooms and a box room. Mel B and Mel C shared one double room, Victoria and Emma shared the other, while Geri had the single. All the girls liked Take That and a poster of the group was put up in the house. They would frequently look at it and say to whoever was around, 'We're going to be bigger than them soon. You wait.'

Shelley said, 'They were a good bunch of girls and they knew how to have a laugh. They were always messing around having fun and wherever they went they seemed to put on a show. Whenever they popped into the pub by the studios, they seemed to take the place over. They were loud and loved causing disruption, but were always funny with it.'

In the beginning, Geri was the only one with a car and her mode of transport brought a few laughs. She had a tiny, ten-year-old pastel-green Fiat Uno. All the girls would squeeze in, giggling and squealing at the lack of space, then drive off, music blaring out, singing and shouting out the window. Two songs they loved at the time were Salt-n-Pepa's 'Let's Talk About Sex' and, appropriately, Cyndi Lauper's 'Girls Just Want To Have Fun'.

When they arrived at the studio, or the house, they would prise themselves out of the car, their limbs aching from the cramped conditions, but still giggling. They were like students on holiday, full of banter and always seeing the funny side of a situation. But the absurdity of the vehicle was matched by the driving. Geri was slightly scatty behind the wheel and easily distracted. The car was always full of noise and chat and her mind constantly raced with ideas. She would often go through red lights unintentionally and had the unnerving habit of driving frighteningly close to parked cars. The car wing mirrors were generally smashed and left hanging limply from the doors, while dents and scratches decorated the bodywork.

Staff at Trinity grew used to the racket outside as the girls pulled up for a day's work. Frequently, Geri would misjudge the tight swinging manoeuvre into the parking spaces and would clunk the front bumper into the wall. There were also many stories about near misses on their travels. After the girls had been to the gym one day, Geri pulled out of a junction a little too quickly and a cyclist crashed into the side, smashing one of the windows. When the girls arrived at the studio, they were seen brushing fragments of diced glass off their clothes, but still giggling.

Another time, they had an accident on the way to work and Chris had to go out to help them. Ian Lee remembered, 'Geri was always hitting kerbs and going through red lights. Her mind was too busy on other things. This time she had blown out two tyres after hitting the kerb and they'd gone off the road on to a green. Apparently, the girls were pretty shaken up, but it wasn't long before they were laughing about it.'

The girls' sense of humour spared no one. Just before Emma joined the group, she had met Mark Verghese in a pub near her home in Finchley and they had started going out together. She was very keen on him and during one weekend when she went home, they slept together for the first time. Naturally, Emma told the girls and when he rang to speak to her a few days later, he was greeted with shouts of 'Well done' from the others in the background. After that initiation, Mark became used to Mel B or Geri grabbing the phone and teasing him with often crude innuendoes.

Almost everyone who came into contact with Touch remembers the wild, anything-goes streak which would become their trademark as the Spice Girls. Neighbours recall the loud music, hysterical laughter and general mayhem coming from the house. The girls got to know some lads living a few doors away after borrowing a cheese grater. Not long after that introduction, Mel B and Geri shocked them by turning up at the front door in long coats, then flashing to reveal they were dressed as sexy St Trinian schoolgirls in short skirts, colourful bras and stockings and suspenders, complete with school ties. The girls were going to a fancy dress party and thought they would give the guys a sneak preview. One of them said, 'We were flabbergasted. They were always full of fun and acting mad.'

Mark Brownsmith was good friends with the owner of the house and he met Mel B for the first time that St Trinian night. He was a strapping fireman who was looking cool in a smart suit for another party. She fancied him and soon after that meeting they began a fling which lasted two months. He later revealed, 'Geri and Mel found out that I was a fireman and they got all giggly and started teasing me about it. They were just like they are now on TV – very loud and over the top. They would come running into the house and go up to people making jokes. They always asked visitors embarrassing questions to get them going. If you could take it, they would leave you alone, but if you went all red, then they would taunt you even more. The girls were always talking about how one day they would be stars, but we never took it seriously.

'Mel would exaggerate her toughness, but I could see through it. She had a very soft side which she covered up and I saw her really upset once. I got on with Mel really well and liked her, but after about two months there was a party at my friend's house and Mel saw me with another girl. We were only having a kiss and a cuddle, but Mel made it clear she wasn't interested after that. Shortly afterwards I saw her with another bloke.'

While Mel B was having boyfriend trouble, Emma and Victoria were both happily in love. Emma's relationship with Mark Verghese became more serious and Victoria was still smitten with fiancé Mark Wood. They kept their relationships secret from Chic, who said they shouldn't get involved for the sake of their careers. Victoria took her engagement ring off whenever he was around, but the money man didn't need to fear his favourite Geri would fall in love. During this period, the girls would tease Geri because she was in a long desert of celibacy.

As the months moved on in the winter, Chic's expenses mounted up and he became tougher with the girls. He continued checking their hours and when Pepi needed to increase the lessons to three times a week, he insisted on sitting in to make sure he was getting his money's-worth. Once he saw how hard they all worked, he stopped coming. But he wasn't happy with their general look and the development of their stage act. He insisted the girls would have to master a half-hour live show before they would be ready, a tall order for a new group. When he saw the choreography to one of their songs, he wasn't impressed and demanded they perform for him every few weeks, so he could monitor their improvement. These little 'gigs' would be nerve-racking moments and the girls would be desperately eager to please. Although he was blunt with them, they appreciated that their chance for pop stardom would not be happening if it wasn't for Chic's money and belief.

Chic couldn't get the Three Degrees story out of his mind. He had capitulated on the leggy black line-up, but he still wanted his girls to have a slick stage act like his old group. One person at Trinity remembers Chic's disquiet and revealed, 'Chic was pretty disgruntled when he saw how they were getting on and he particularly didn't like their choreography. After one routine, he said to the girls, "Nah, nah, nah. You ain't moving right – it's all wrong." He then got up and started to show them how he thought it should be done. He jigged about, clicking his fingers, moving backwards and forwards. It was hilarious. There was this man in his fifties, with heavy jewellery and grey hair, telling these young girls how to dance. All the girls had to turn away and not look at each other because they knew they would crack up laughing. It was so daft.

'Emma, Victoria and Mel C used to go home at weekends which annoyed Chic. It also made Geri angry. She would try to make them stay at the house, so they could keep working. Chic used to say, "How are you going to get anywhere if you don't work all the time? Why aren't you working weekends? You can't just clock off in this game. You've got to work, work, work and only then will you get better. You are very lucky girls. You have got this opportunity, but you've got to work harder." He was tough like that, but he was spending a fortune keeping them going, so he had a right to expect the best out of them.'

But Chic wasn't all bad. He continued to cover all their bills and expenses and occasionally treated them to lavish nights out. The girls would leave the little Fiat Uno and hop into Chic's blue convertible Rolls Royce to head into the West End, where he would take them for dinner at a smart restaurant and then on to one of the many casinos he was known at. For the girls, it was a one of their earliest glimpses of the glamorous world of money and they loved every expensive minute.

Although Touch failed to impress Chic, they did stir some appreciation in those formative months. Trinity Studios is a non-profit-making organisation set up by a charitable trust to help develop local talent. While the girls rehearsed there, they gave two performances for various people. The first was an impromptu rendition of two numbers for nine leisure service engineers from the local council who were being guided round the building by Ian Lee. He introduced them to the girls, who gladly sang two songs: 'We're Gonna Make It Happen' and 'Take Me Away'. They earnt themselves keen applause and some much needed encouragement. The next performance was at an open day organised to show off the facilities at Trinity. It was attended by local dignitaries including Woking MP Sir Cranley Onslow. Again, the girls were a hit. It may have been only a tiny audience, but it was live and appreciative and was better than playing to their reflections in the giant mirror, or to Chic, who they knew deeply wished they were taller and darker.

Shelley D'Silva was at the open-day gig. She said, 'They had only been rehearsing for a few months and I was amazed how much they had improved. I had seen them at the auditions and the change was incredible. They had good dance routines and they sounded great. They went down really well and I remember thinking to myself, These girls can do it, they're going to be famous. They had worked so hard and were so ambitious. They were so hungry for fame you couldn't help but want them to make it.'

Those two performances may have been fun, but they weren't enough for the girls. They were impatient to move on and wanted to write and record new material, not continually churn out five songs which weren't even written for them. This became an enduring bone of contention between the girls and the management and it continued to fester. They got bored with the same songs and would ask Pepi to let them work on others, but she refused to move on until they had perfected their basic training.

None of the girls could play instruments, apart from Mel B who was good on the drums, but they would emerge as good lyricists. One of their early attempts, however, was a disaster. They went to record a demo tape of 'We're Gonna Make It Happen' at Erwin Keiles's house. It was their first recording experience, but the day started badly when they presented Erwin and his partner with some new lyrics to the song. The girls had written a rap section which they felt made the song more suitable to their style and age, but the two writers were horrified. Erwin said, 'They felt some of our words weren't quite what young girls would say, so they had gone ahead and re-written a couple of lines. We were quite upset they had messed around with our song and I told them that wasn't the way things were done in this business. You can't just take someone's song and change it. I said it was fine if they wanted things altered, then it could be done properly. We really liked the rap, but one of their lines didn't even make English sense. In the end, we changed it collectively and they were thrilled. They were really enthusiastic about being in the studio and you could tell they thought this was another big step for them. They were quite giggly, but they got down to the work and we spent about six hours recording. Geri seemed to be the one who organised them all. We recorded it digitally, so the quality was excellent and when we played back the finished song they thought it was fantastic.'

Another early experience in the studio came at Trinity where Ian Lee brought the girls in to record a jingle for some training videos he was working on for a company called Perfect Vision. They simply harmonised the name of the company, but the few hours in the studio was a bit of light relief from the monotony of rehearsing.

As the group's act became more professional, Chris announced they were ready to perform a showcase gig for songwriters and music publishers. The objective was to find proven writers to work with the girls and build an album's-worth of material. The writing would take many months, but once it was complete, they would be in a strong position to approach record companies and secure a lucrative deal. The girls could easily release a cover version, a route taken by most boy bands, but Chic and the Herberts were adamant that the only way to ensure longevity was for the girls to have original material.

Rehearsals continued with renewed pressure in the lead up to the showcase, which was scheduled for the beginning of December. The work load produced a slight scare a few weeks before the event when Mel C had to have her tonsils out after suffering repeated sore throats. Her voice had deteriorated after so much singing and she became very upset, fearing she would be sacked. But the operation solved her problems and she made a speedy recovery.

To chronicle the build-up to the showcase and the rise of the group generally, a camera crew from Rave Productions was hired to make a fly-on-the-wall documentary of the road to fame. The girls were filmed rehearsing at Trinity and interviewed about their hopes for the future. Sitting on a red plastic chair in the dance studio, they took it in turns to reveal their thoughts. Victoria was the one who looked the most different from her current Spice Girl look. Back then, she had long hair and was noticeably heavier, a long way from her slim Posh Spice figure – and she even smiled for the camera! She said innocently, 'We are all working really, really hard. We are all really ambitious, which is good, and none of us are really that lazy.

We want to just carry on doing it and we want to be in *Smash Hits* and on *Top Of The Pops* and things like that.' Emma spoke in a soft voice, 'My ambition is obviously to make it really big. I think we are all great and we can do it if we work hard. I hope we can keep working together and getting on really, really well.'

Both girls seemed shy and nervous, but Geri was super-confident. She turned the chair back to front as she spoke and had the nerve to talk openly about the man who was bank rolling the group. She said, 'I think Chic is a very, very clever man and I don't think anyone should underestimate him. He has been there and he gives a lot of chat about the Three Degrees – I'm sure you will hear this story a hundred times. His ideas are good, but they're just dated, that's all.' Then, banging her right hand on the back of the chair and gripping it tightly, she added, 'I'm quite a motivated, enthusiastic person. My time is running out – I've *got* to get there. I'm quite hungry for fame – I need my ego fed.'

Geri was only twenty-two when she gave that interview, yet she was convinced her best years to find fame were passing by. As far as she was concerned, she had waited long enough for stardom and now it was within sight she wanted to make that final grab as soon as possible. She wanted action and she wanted it now. This was the root of the problems between the group and their first managers and that interview clearly showed the signs of unrest which would eventually kill off Touch and breathe life into the Spice Girls.

– 8 –

SWITCHING ON GIRL POWER

During the build-up to the showcase, the frustration became more noticeable in the girls, particularly in Geri and Mel B. The management started watching run-throughs at Trinity, and Mel B would deliberately only go through the motions during certain numbers, giving the minimum of input. If she was pulled up by whoever was watching and asked to put in more effort, her frequent retort was, 'I don't have to, I can pull it out of the bag on the day, I can do it when I have to.'

As they worked through November, Mel B's delinquent attitude and Geri's mounting anger spread through the group like an epidemic until they all became restless. The dissatisfaction evolved out of their own growing strength. They had been practising since June together, and since September with Emma, and they knew now that they had something good going. Their singing had improved immeasurably with Pepi's lessons, and their dance routines were sexy and slick. Above all, they had become good friends. They shared ambition and belief in themselves and they were prepared to work hard for what they wanted. In the beginning, Geri and Mel B had repelled each other like two positive electrical charges because they were too similar. But over the months they had became close. They spent weekends going to parties, raves and clubs together while the others went off with their boyfriends or back to their families. During that extra time, those two forceful personalities had fused to create one super-powerful charge and it now wanted to take control of Touch.

Pepi Lemer had fallen into a sort of unofficial mothering role as she got closer to the girls. She had taken them out for many breakfasts and lunches and cooked them healthy meals when they came for lessons at her house. She had even given them the odd item of clothing from her wardrobe and remembers giving Geri a pink jacket. During breaks in the lessons, they chatted about everyday things – boyfriends, families, fashion, whatever was in the day's news – and then the girls confided in her about their fears for the future. Pepi remembered, 'They were terribly frustrated and not happy. Geri in particular wanted things to move faster. She was saying, "We've got to do something. Chic is old-fashioned. We've got to leave these guys, go on our own. Nothing is happening – this is our time we're wasting. We've got to look out for other people." She was being very forceful and determined.

'I remember saying to them that they should take power for themselves. If they weren't happy about something they should phone the guys, call meetings and discuss the problems formally, get them sorted out. I suggested they should write down everything they required and what they wanted for the future. Be professional, I said, don't be manipulated, you don't have to do anything you don't want to do. I used the word "power" quite a few times. I think I was simply reiterating what they already knew, but I had put it in a more mature way. Geri had certainly sussed it for herself already.

'Not long after that, Mel B started writing things down and the girls had meetings with Chic, Bob and Chris. It was Geri and Mel B who did all the talking and they were quite forceful – they really put their case across. One day, they were all having a heated argument in the kitchen at the house. Bob was asking them what they wanted to change and the girls were saying that things were going too slowly. He told them, "You can't rush because you're not ready." They clearly thought they were.

'Once, I remember us talking about fate and things happening because they are meant to. I said, All you can do is your best, be as ambitious and as powerful as you can and go for it. They were so hungry for success and I remember looking at these incredibly ambitious faces and saying to them, You can be the bees knees, you can be Stevie Wonder and Celine Dion all tied up in one, but that doesn't mean you are going to make it. There are no guarantees, not in this business. This game is like a lottery, girls. Only one in a hundred million makes it and, no matter how good you are, you still have to be very lucky.'

These were wise words indeed and luck may well prove to have been the deciding factor. But, for Geri, she wanted the power to *make* their own luck.

The showcase was scheduled for 7 December at NOMIS. Shortly before the big day, the girls performed a complete dress rehearsal of their gig for the management, Pepi and the staff at Trinity. It was a great success. Pepi felt very proud and Chris and Bob seemed happy. In fact, everyone was impressed, except Chic, who was still not sure they were ready. Whatever Chic said, it couldn't be denied that Chris Herbert's dream had taken shape. A year earlier, he had begun trawling the streets and dance colleges of Britain with those flyers and a head full of ideas. Now, as those around him could see, he had created a singing and dancing group to be proud of. Sure, they needed some fine-tuning and maybe a little styling, but, most importantly, they were ready for Phase Two. As Chris confirmed on the group's video documentary, the showcase was the next critical step forward in his master plan. It would forge partnerships in which the girls could write their own songs. Out of those songs, their style and attitude would shine through and prepare them for their big launch.

The night before the showcase, Shelley went to Boyn Hill Road to discuss what the girls would wear for the performance. As a stylist, she could offer advice on the image they should project, but she admits now that they didn't need much help because they had already decided. They had chosen very casual clothes – jeans or dark trousers, except sporty Mel C who wore black tracksuits bottoms. Geri, Victoria and Mel B chose different coloured tight Adidas T-shirts – shortened to leave bare midriffs for Geri and Mel B. Mel C and Emma wore white vests. Mel B and Emma also wore Kangol caps turned back-to-front, although Emma's cream cap looked slightly too big. They agreed with Shelley that they should all dress fairly neutrally, so one girl wouldn't stand out, which could misdirect the focus. It could make the writers think Touch had a lead singer with a backing group.

On the day of the showcase, the girls asked Pepi to meet them at NOMIS to take them through some warm-up exercises. She also brought along her daughter, Dani, a qualified beautician, to help with their make-up. At first Mel C said she didn't want make-up because she had once been told it didn't suit her, but she then agreed to have a light base so that she didn't look like a ghost next to the others.

The girls were pumped up with adrenalin for the crunch day and it showed in their performance. It was energetic and near faultless. They sang confidently and executed their dance moves slickly. Mel C showed off her back-flip during one number, but they saved their best routine for after the gig. It was then that the girls' true charm and wit bubbled over. They flirted and joked with the writers and, basically, began networking like true pros.

Erwin Keiles was there with his songwriting partner John Thirkell. He said, 'They went down really well and it became known that they were our songs the girls were singing, so we got approached by various people that day, too. The girls were going round speaking to people and we were within earshot sometimes. They were talking as if they'd already had their first million seller and were now busy looking for songwriters to write their next album with them. They had such incredible self-belief. They were so confident and cheeky that anyone would have thought they already had a big record deal, yet they were complete novices.'

The showcase was a resounding success and the girls made a big impression on a number of key people who would greatly influence their future. Many writers said they were keen to work with them and the feedback was overwhelmingly positive. It was everything the girls wanted to hear after so many months of singing to empty rooms and a big mirror. To have encouragement from respected people at the heart of the business was invaluable and the prospects were very exciting. It was also exactly what the management wanted to hear and, in the weeks that followed, they began booking up sessions with some writers. Little did Chris and Bob know then that introducing their girls to the music industry would precipitate their own demise.

The mood seemed to change after the showcase. The girls' confidence was boosted and they became more independent and less insecure. In the weeks running up to Christmas there seemed to be a definite shift in control, which the people at Trinity could sense. The girls had become a very cliquey gang and Geri was firmly entrenched as the leader, with Mel B as her chief of staff. The group was now fuelling itself and they didn't want to be bossed around any more. They organised their own gig for the pupils at Emma's mum's karate school in Finchley. It was only for youngsters, but the show was a hit and further boosted morale.

The girls had their last lesson with Pepi shortly before Christmas. It only came about because Geri, sharp as ever, had kept track of all the lessons and noticed they were still owed two hours. Rather than let it go and get on with the festive spirit, she called and suggested they come for the tuition at Pepi's house. They sang well and seemed buoyant with optimism for the future. Once the lesson was over, they gave Pepi a card with the message: 'Thanks for everything, we couldn't have done it without you.' They then hugged her and she wished them all good luck. 'We weren't like best buddies, but I felt we had become quite close,' Pepi said. 'I had seen them put so much in over all those months. They were hungry as hell to be stars and you couldn't help but want them to make it.'

That Christmas, Emma, Mel C and Victoria went back to their various families and boyfriends while Geri and Mel B went on a cheap holiday to Gran Canaria. It was a mark of their deep friendship that they would go on holiday at such a family-oriented time. The future of the group would have certainly been a prime subject of debate on that holiday, in between the wild partying. And, without doubt, the two girls would have agreed it was time that Girl Power seized control of Touch.

Following the Christmas and New Year celebrations, the girls regrouped at Boyn Hill Road and the management began finalising recording sessions with writers from the showcase. At this time, the girls were also introduced to writers Richard Stannard and Matthew Rowe, better known in the business as Biff and Matt. They all clicked instantly and it would prove to be one of the most critical partnerships in the girls' careers. It was with Biff and Matt that they would go on to write several of their massive hits, including 'Wannabe' and '2 Become 1'.

Another songwriter and musician who worked with the girls during this period was Tim Hawes who was based at Trinity. He saw the girls' early talent for songwriting develop, and he also witnessed the disintegration of their relationship with their first managers. Tim had got to know the girls in the run-up to the showcase and had worked with them in the studio on some material. He had written a song called 'Sugar And Spice', but had only completed the chorus when he started working on it with the girls. Tim explained, 'We worked together on that song for quite a few days. The girls had been trying for ages to think of a name for the group because they weren't happy with Touch. They were coming up with loads of ideas, but they couldn't settle on anything. I thought Spice would be a good name and in the middle of one session I said, "How about using Spice as a name?" They all seemed to take to it quite quickly. They all went, "Umm, yeah, that could be OK." It was nothing more dramatic than that. They chewed it over for a while and really seemed to like it. Chris came into the studio later and they told him they were going to call themselves Spice and he liked it too. I really didn't think about it again and the girls never mentioned it either.

'They were very good in the studio and their ideas for lyrics and melodies are probably second to none. We would sit down with a pen and paper and work through with a backing track I had written playing constantly. When I worked with them, I would say Geri was the greatest contributor on the lyrics side, without any doubt. On the songs we did, she probably wrote 60–70 per cent of the lyrics. She wasn't the one to come up with the tune, but she was good at writing accessible pop lyrics with wide appeal. Mel B was also good at lyrics and Mel C was by far the best singer and was good at melodies. I wrote another song called "Is This Love" and, because I loved her voice, Mel C sang it for me as a favour and the other girls did some backing vocals.'

Tim completed two songs with the girls, but it was the third which caused problems and remained unfinished. The girls didn't like it and when the management insisted they record it, they weren't happy. As far as they were concerned, the time had come for them to develop their own style. They had put up with songs they didn't particularly like for long enough, now was the time to sing what *they* wanted.

The song was just one matter among several which the girls were unhappy about. There were also tense negotiations about a contract during the first couple of months of 1995. There had been no formal deal up until now, even though the girls had wanted one, because Chic was reluctant to sign an agreement until he was convinced they were fully ready. When a contract was finally discussed, the girls weren't as interested any more. By this time, they had started to have their own ideas about their future. Ian Lee remembered, 'The girls would talk to Tim and me regularly about the contract problems – they were unhappy about the deal they were being offered. They only had a gentleman's agreement up until then, but then the management finally offered a deal which would tie them for five years. The girls were worried about the length of time. They asked me what I thought and it did strike me as too long. Normally, contracts are about two or three years with options.'

The problem simmered while the girls continued with their various writing sessions. All the time they were gaining confidence and being told they had the talent to make it. Geri was at the fore-front of any confrontation with the management. Tim Hawes said, 'Geri was quite outspoken and I'm convinced that if she and Melanie Brown hadn't been in the group, they would never have broken away. Geri's ambitious streak made her valuable to the band and Chris and Bob probably saw her as a threat to their security because she was starting to call the shots.

'If there was a discussion, Geri would always be the one to stand up to Chris. She was the mouthpiece for the band. At the very beginning, Geri and Mel didn't get on too well because they are both domineering, but they became close friends and when you combined the two of them, they became quite a lethal weapon.'

The crunch came during the last week of February and the beginning of March. The disagreements about recording the song with Tim had continued. As the events were to unfold, it's clear the girls had made their decision to break away from the management team prior to this period. The staff at Trinity noticed the girls didn't turn up for work as usual and no one knew where they were. On Friday, 3 March, the girls officially took control of the group. Tim Hawes and Ian Lee were at Trinity when the final act of the girls' stay there was played out. Tim recalled, 'We had been working on the song the girls didn't like. Chris was pushing them to write and sing it, but the girls weren't happy. That seemed to be the lowest point. The girls felt all along that they were having songs pushed on them. They did Erwin Keiles's songs when they arrived because they were new and eager to please. Once they had become a bonded group, they had a united power and they wanted to make their own decisions and didn't want Chris and Bob plotting their future.

'During the last two weeks I reckon they were just planning how they would disappear and making sure they had copies of all the songs they had done, so they could use them to promote themselves to other companies.

'The girls came in to the studio that Friday afternoon. I had been given instructions not to give them any backing tracks or finished versions of the songs we had done. There was clearly an air of suspicion with regard to what the girls were up to. Geri came up around lunchtime and basically charmed the backing tracks out of me. She said they wanted to work out their dance routines. I ended up giving her the "Sugar And Spice" tapes.

'Ten to fifteen minutes after that, there was a scene downstairs which, beyond any question, was staged. They had a big argument. The gist of it was that they couldn't work together anymore. It was schoolgirl stuff and obvious that it was a mock up. I thought that at the time because it was over dramatic, far too over the top. They stormed out of the building shouting at each other and that was it. They were gone and no one saw anything of them again. It all suddenly fell into place. They had reclaimed all the bits they needed to go and promote themselves and they obviously weren't going to hang around.'

That was the last anyone at Trinity and the managers saw of the five girls. Later, the Boyn Hill Road house was found empty and neighbours just recall the girls giving a celebratory beep of their car horns as they drove off. The next communication from the girls was a solicitor's letter saying they wanted to end their connection with Chic, Chris and Bob formally. It was a sad and brutal end to the business relationship, but the final legal conclusion would be settled amicably for all parties many months later.

It was the end of a dream for the three men, and particularly so for Chris. His five girls had been perfect on all the original four counts he had searched for: they were Streetwise, Outgoing, Ambitious and Dedicated. But he hadn't planned on all those adding up to one all encompassing factor – Girl Power.

– 9 –

GONNABEES

As Chris, Bob and Chic licked their wounds and counted the financial, as well as emotional, costs of their venture, the newly named group Spice revelled in its new-found freedom. The girls kept an appointment with the writer Eliot Kennedy, which had been arranged before their hasty departure from Trinity. It was a fruitful session which marked the beginning of a positive partnership. He would eventually be credited with writing two songs on the début album, including 'Love Thing' and the smash hit 'Say You'll Be There', so it was certainly good news for Kennedy they had made that meeting!

In the following months, the girls kept up a relentless pace, networking with their contacts, writing songs and preparing demo tapes which would lead them to a new management team and a big record deal. They worked with Stannard and Rowe and it was during this time that they wrote 'Wannabe', the aptly titled song that would answer their dreams and change all their lives.

Geri was firmly in control and kept a keen eye on the girls. She was as tough and demanding as any of the previous managers had been. When Victoria went away for a weekend with her boyfriend, Mark, Geri got very angry. The girls were meant to record 'Wannabe', so she called Victoria's home repeatedly. Victoria got so upset that her mum stepped in and told Geri they were in a pop group, not a 'religious cult'. Victoria did go away for the weekend, but it wasn't long before her relationship with Mark ended and she pledged her faith to the group.

If the girls thought it would be a swift route into the charts after leaving their first managers, they were wrong. It would take a while to find a manager they were happy with and, at times, it must have been frustrating and worrying. They had walked out on a management team who had been backing them all the way and providing them with a home, to a life of freedom, but one which was edged with acute uncertainty. They met many record industry executives to sing *a cappella* for them, but a record deal wasn't forthcoming. Emma even introduced them to her former acting agent.

The girls' nerve finally paid off when they were introduced to Simon Fuller, the man who would turn their pop star fantasy into stunning reality. Fuller was already a hugely successful music manager long before he met Spice. He had started in the music business working for Chrysalis records before quitting to manage a bright young musician called Paul Hardcastle. In 1985, Hardcastle had a British No. 1 and world-wide hit with the quirky single 'Nineteen'. Fuller formed a management company under the same name and went on to develop several top acts. He turned Cathy Dennis into an international star and guided Annie Lennox's solo career. But, for a man behind such high-profile stars, surprisingly little is known about Fuller. He is now in his mid thirties and people who have met him say he is a modest, unassuming man, who prefers that his artists take the full glare of the spotlight and not him. What is known, however, is that Fuller has a sharp eye for talent and an adept skill, matched with the right world-wide connections, particularly in America, for maximising all potential. Immediately he heard the Spice demos he saw a group with something special and signed them to 19 Management. He then proved his golden touch beyond question by taking the wheel and steering their meandering careers on an immaculate and direct route to super-stardom.

By September 1995, Fuller had secured a huge contract for the girls with Virgin Records. The advance alone was reported to be £500,000. It was a truly remarkable turn around. Less than a year before, the girls had been slogging it out at Trinity, still dreaming of making a record. Now, it was going to happen. Soon after this deal was signed, a financial settlement was reached with the previous managers to compensate them for their time and money spent developing the group. The details of the deal have always remained strictly confidential, but people at Trinity who know the men say they were content with the agreement and harbour no bitterness towards the girls. They are philosophical rather than bitter and, as far as they are concerned, they put the ingredients of the group together, but the girls made themselves.

As the girls, Fuller and Virgin planned the strategy for the group's development and launch, they were faced with one immediate problem – the name Spice. Unfortunately, it was already being used by an American rapper, so it had to be changed. It isn't clear who suggested the vital addition to the name, but the transformation from unwanted wannabees to fated gonnabees with a record deal was complete when they became the Spice Girls.

On 14 October, the new group was proudly invited by Charisma Records – a subsidiary of Virgin – to a race meeting at Kempton Park, in Surrey, where the company had sponsored a Gold Cup steeplechase for twenty-two years. The girls were guests of honour for the day. A horse race meeting seemed an odd place to parade a pop group, but maybe it was to emphasise how they saw the Spice Girls – as a thoroughbred in the Virgin stable of talent. Whatever the reasons, the girls certainly showed that day how their race to the top would be run: loud, wild and humorously. Their first publicity photocall was in front of the bronze statue of the legendary race-horse Desert Orchid. It was a twee publicity idea: legend of the track meets legends-to-be of pop. It should have made a sweet picture with a few kind paragraphs in some of the newspapers. That is until the Spice Girls hijacked the photocall in what would become their own inimitable style. As the photographers captured the scripted shot, the girls took the reins of the proceedings and started climbing all over the sacred statue. Some racegoers and stewards looked on in utter disgust. Who on earth did these young fillies think they were, fooling around on the monument to one of the greatest steeplechasers of all time? It was bad form indeed.

The spiced-up version of the photocall caused a mini uproar and, as a result, received some tabloid newspaper coverage the next day, as well as making the local television bulletins. The girls proved that when it comes to running in the publicity stakes, like Desert Orchid, they are second to none.

The buzz about Virgin's hot new signing had already swept through the music business and the pop media. As 1996 began, it was now time to spread that word throughout Britain and the world. A master plan was set in motion to generate the hype around the group in the lead up to the release of 'Wannabe'. It would be a long, controlled and truly brilliant campaign.

The girls were taken to the annual Brit Awards ceremony in London. Obviously, they weren't up for any trophies, but it was a way for Virgin to show them off and it was all part of keeping the buzz going. It was a fantastic experience for the girls, even though few people took any real notice of them: after all, new acts are signed all the time with big promises of being the next big thing – why should these girls be any different?

The 'Wannabe' video was shot in St Pancras, North London. The girls deliberately steered away from the overtly sexual images portrayed by previous girl bands. They wanted it to be off-beat, wacky, with a spontaneous vibe and be full of humour. Basically, they wanted it to reflect the attitude of the group and the song. The video had a trial airing on the music channel *The Box* and instantly struck a chord with viewers. It proved so popular that Vincent Monsey, chief executive of the station, scaled up its screening priority level so that it was played seventy times a week. He said, 'When I saw the Spice Girls, their personalities came right through and I knew they would do something big. They had self-propelling talent.'

Self-propelling they certainly were, but one fear in the early days was that the group wouldn't get the much-needed support of the teen press. Traditionally, the key magazines were reluctant to run stories on all-girl bands, so the girls were sent to woo the editors. There were no better ambassadors to the Spice Girls' cause than the girls themselves. Among the executives they met were the editors of *Smash Hits* and *Top Of The Pops* magazine. The girls sang 'Wannabe' to a backing tape and *a cappella* versions of songs on the album. More importantly, they blitzed the editors with their person-alities and the ethos of Girl Power. They explained that they weren't just another one-dimensional girl group, they had something to say and were a group with attitude who were *for* the girls, as much as the boys.

The editor of *Top Of The Pops* magazine, Peter Loraine, was impressed when he met the girls over lunch in Notting Hill, West London. They sang *a cappella* and later did a photo shoot for the magazine. It was during lunch he suggested giving each Spice Girl a nickname. It was a fun idea, but no one knew then just how it would catch on. Peter said, 'We were talking about the launch of the single and their image and they told me everything they had planned. They said they would release "Wannabe", then another single, then the next, then the album. They said they were going to America. It was all laid out, nothing was left to chance. They knew exactly what they were doing and knew it was all going to work.

'I simply said that it would be a good idea if they had some nicknames. The girls liked the idea, so I had an editorial meeting back at the office and about four of us started thinking of names. Posh was the first one to be thought up because Victoria looked pretty sophisticated. The rest were pretty easy really because the girls' characters were already so strong. The names jumped out at us. We laughed the most when we came up with Scary. Jennifer Cawthron, who was also from Leeds, came up with that one because Mel B was so loud and had tried to take over the whole photo shoot.

'We ran with the names for a couple of issues and the first time the girls saw them they thought it was very funny. Then the newspapers started picking up on the names and they cropped up everywhere until they were fully accepted by everyone.'

As the countdown to the release of 'Wannabe' began, a full-page advert appeared in an early July edition of *Smash Hits*. It indicated the kind of confidence that was behind the girls even before they had secured a hit. The ad was like a formal declaration of the Spice Girls' imminent dominance of world pop. It read: *'Wanted: Anyone with a sense of fun, freedom, and adventure. Hold tight, get ready – Girl Power is comin' at you.'* In the light of what was to follow, it was by no means an overstatement.

'Wannabe' was released during the second week of July and went straight in at No. 3, sparking interest from national newspapers, which until then had been wary of the hype. Geri said, 'This song is like us – you'll either love it or hate it. It'll do nothing or go all the way. There is a big campaign behind us and we are hoping to be even bigger than Eternal by this time next year.' But Victoria set the tone for the future when she said, 'Whatever happens to us, I just want to make sure we enjoy every minute of it. Let's just say that Cyndi Lauper could have written "Girls Just Want To Have Fun" with us in mind!' When she said that, the girls had already come a long way from the days when they screamed that song while enjoying a white-knuckle ride in Geri's Fiat Uno. And the distance from those humble beginnings would soon become immeasurable.

In its second week, 'Wannabe' went to No. 1 and gave the girls their first record-breaking musical landmark by becoming the first all-female group to have a No. 1 hit with their début single. Victoria was cautious about the achievement and said, 'We're as shocked as everyone else by the success of "Wannabe". It doesn't put us under any pressure to follow it up. If it's the only No. 1 we ever have, at least it proves what we're capable of. It's brilliant because it was the public who put it there, so it shows they enjoy what we do, but it's still just a paper fact about record sales. It's only one tiny step for us as a band. We've already recorded an album which we're incredibly proud of and that's what we're really anxious for people to get into.'

Ironically, 'Wannabe' stole the limelight from two former Take That heart-throbs who were launching their solo careers. Firstly, it replaced Gary Barlow's début solo single, 'Forever Love', at No. 1 and the following week, it held on to the No. 1 position, forcing Robbie Williams to settle for No. 2 with his cover version of George Michael's 'Freedom'. Girl Power had easily stood the first test against Boy Power.

Mel C said at the time, 'Going to No. 1 hasn't sunk in for us yet. We've been working so hard for the last two years. It's a great compliment to be compared to Take That because they were so successful for such a long time. But we are different. They were controlled by a management team – we're on our own. At the end of the day we all write our own stuff. We are not Take That, we are Spice

Girls.' Geri echoed that sentiment when she added, 'We're not some kind of concept. We call the shots. I don't want to put men down, but it's time for some strong females. Girl Power!'

'Wannabe' continued to hold its No. 1 position in the UK and began hitting the top spots across Europe. As the Spice Girls' success snowballed, so did the media interest. Suddenly magazines and newspapers wanted to hear what the girls had to say and they proved to be naturals at providing good headlines. For so long, teen magazines and the pop press had been stupefied by the banal, goody-goody image of boy bands who would avoid saying anything which might cause a stir. The Spice Girls were the direct opposite to that and crushed the mould with one heavy stamp of their platform shoes. They didn't care what they said or whose feathers they ruffled, just as long as they got a reaction. They were a welcome breath of fresh air.

Victoria said, 'Spice Girls is about taking 1960s feminism and dressing it up for the 1990s. It's more than just another girl group. Women have to shout louder than men to be heard and our music is great because it gives us an extremely loud voice. Our aim is to be an inspiration to other girls. We're about unity and solidarity between female friends. We're also about freedom of expression, which is why we wanted to retain our own personalities. We don't need a uniform to show we have something in common. There's a message in our madness. We also have a sense of humour, integrity and passion.'

And Mel C chipped in, 'To be a feminist in the 1990s means having something to say for yourself. You can wear mascara and high heels and look like a babe and make as much of a point as if you shaved your head and burnt your bra. There's no way I'm ever burning my Wonderbra. I couldn't – I'm nothing without it.'

By the end of July, Spice Girls mania had already hit a dozen countries. Japan was one of the first to really take off, so the girls flew there to promote the single and it soon rose to No. 1. From then on, fan hysteria, media frenzy and No. 1 hit after hit greeted the girls at every destination. They were mobbed everywhere they went and Girl Power truly began to leave its scorch mark across the globe.

The Spice Girls were dubbed 'Oasis with a Wonderbra' to which they replied, 'Nah, Oasis are Spice Girls in drag!' The girls certainly seemed capable of causing as much trouble as the 'Mad for it' Manchester band. The 'Wannabe' video was banned in certain parts of South-east Asia because Mel B's nipples were too prominent. In Japan they virtually took over the *Space Shower* show when they ambushed the two male presenters, who complained, 'This is our show, not theirs!' The Spice Girls' ambush would become the girls' familiar calling card. They inflicted it on Boyzone's Stephen Gately by teasing him remorselessly at a pop festival in Germany, and on French TV they smeared a congratulatory cake over the faces of other guests.

There were also reports of Victoria flashing open her dressing-gown to a lift full of people in a hotel in Holland and, in another hotel, Mel B ran down the corridor naked. At Glasgow airport in Scotland, Geri tried on some sexy underwear at the Sock Shop and stunned an assistant by strutting around the shop half naked, while back in London the girls brought some sneers when they jeered Kula Shaker at *Top Of The Pops*.

To the unsuspecting world, all these daft antics were new, but to the girls it was just a wider audience for the behaviour which had evolved during those mad months getting to know one another in Boyn Hill Road. The gang always enjoyed a good party – and this was the best bash they'd ever been to.

'Wannabe' stayed at the top in Britain for seven weeks and sold more than one million copies. Despite having just one hit, the girls were already being hailed as a phenomenon and there seemed no fear among the fans and the media that it was a fluke. Even serious newspapers such as *The Times* were quick to support them, one article proclaiming, 'Their pop songs are smart and sharp, the band fill a gap in the UK music market with fun and flair and harness their pro-girl attitude with a spot-on sense of humour.'

In September, the girls flew to America to shoot the video to the second single, 'Say You'll Be There', in the Mojave desert. They saw Jon Bon Jovi on a running machine in the gym at their hotel and, in typical Spice Girls fashion, they were brutally honest and admitted, 'He's not as nice looking in real life, is he?' They were equally disappointed when they saw Bryan Adams and realised he was so 'dinky' in the flesh.

During this trip, Geri had her first tattoo, a jaguar cat on the base of her spine in memory of her dad, because he used to drive a Jaguar car. The heartache that the man who had inspired her self-motivation wasn't alive to see her make it, became ever more acute for Geri with the band's growing success.

On 21 October, 'Say You'll Be There' went straight to No. 1 in the UK, replacing Boyzone's cover version, 'Words'. It revved the Spice Girls hype into another gear. The only bad news came when a soft-porn magazine published the nude photographs of Geri – giving the magazine its biggest ever sale of 150,000. The pictures were quickly bought by a tabloid newspaper, and Geri's breasts were suddenly on show to millions. Later, one photo was blown up into a giant poster and sold in Athena shops. Geri had feared the pictures would turn up as soon as she became famous. She had shown the girls the snaps when they were living in Maidenhead, so she wasn't surprised and now laughed it off. She said, 'I thought it was funny – my boobs look good though, didn't they? I'm sure people see me as a screaming redhead with a big pair of boobs, but I like to think I've got things to say.'

Also in October, the album *Spice* was released in Japan and went to No. 1 with reports that sales were outstripping records set by the Beatles at their peak. Even back in the UK, the singles were still selling hundreds of thousands and the Spice Girls fan club was receiving 10,000 applications each week.

In November, Virgin laid on a party for the UK launch of the album, *Spice,* at a restaurant overlooking the River Thames on the South Bank. At the start, the girls were awarded a framed disc of 'Wannabe' to mark three million sales world-wide and it was confirmed it had now reached No. 1 in twenty-two countries. Then the girls plunged a model detonator and set off a £65,000 fireworks display over the London skyline. As the extravagant colours and flashes lit the night, the girls could be heard cracking jokes – 'Ooooh, that was a car! Aaaah, there goes a holiday. Urrrrgh, all that could have bought a house!' Whatever the gags, the girls were truly stunned by their success, yet still maintained a grip on reality. Geri said, 'We could be in the gutter tomorrow. What isn't real to me is selling three million copies of "Wannabe". OK, so a lot of people think Girl Power is a load of cheese, but if we can give anyone a bit of motivation, make any girl just sit up and go, "I'm strong", then that beats any No. 1, or meeting any star.'

Mel B admitted, 'You don't really accept what is happening to you. You can get caught up in the hyper vibe, but you just have to re-adjust yourself. I think people can tell we aren't up our own bottoms. You can see people who are like, "Yeah, I'm Number One!" Arggh! They're the ones you want to smack in the face!'

The album had advance orders alone of more than 500,000, which ensured it was an instant hit. It went to No. 1 in the UK and all across Europe, and the reviews, as much as the sales, boosted the girls' confidence and profile. Many boy band albums had been clev-erly knitted together with a mix of cover versions of proven chart hits and original songs written by other musicians, but all ten tracks on *Spice* were collaborations with the Spice Girls and a mix of writers.

One music critic on *The Times* was certainly impressed and wrote, 'The editor of *Smash Hits* called them "Oasis with a Wonderbra", and she could be right. For while Oasis have forged mainstream pop from the crucible of "serious" rock'n'roll, the Spice Girls are travelling in the opposite direction, taking a pure pop formula and giving it a surprisingly credible edge. Their reward may well be success, and possibly respect on a scale to rival that of Oasis. It is tempting to dismiss *Spice* on first hearing as just another frothy confection for the kids. Like all good pop it has an air of energetic frivolity, and more bounce than beat. But you do not have to be a pre-pubescent girl to appreciate the genuine sense of resolve that runs like a thin thread of steel through the ten tracks. Peppered with slogans such as "I'm choosy, not a floozy", the album has a constantly assertive ring about it, yet always favouring guile and wit above aggression. And on "Naked", a slow song full of sexual tension, in which a voice on a telephone insists "I'd rather be hated than pitied", they hint at a depth of feeling that goes well beyond the superficial charm of traditional teen-pop.'

It was quite an accolade to have a fan base of pre-teen and teenage boys and girls, yet still command the respect of the 'serious' music critics. Normally, coverage of a teen band is restricted to pop magazines and the tabloid showbiz columns, with the normal spattering of TV interviews on youth programmes, but the Spice Girls were transgressing all media barriers. They were perceived to be influencing a generation of youngsters and their Girl Power slogan had significance which reflected a social change of some kind. Their success was being analysed as more than just another big chart act.

The wide-ranging appeal in the girls was graphically highlighted at the annual *Smash Hits* Poll Winners' Party in December at the London Arena. The girls performed 'Wannabe' and 'Say You'll Be There' for a screaming audience and collected three awards – Best British Group, Best New Act and Best Video for 'Say You'll Be There'.

Mel C said, 'I used to watch it on telly and dreamed about winning an award, so it's a dream come true. I've been on the cover of *Smash Hits* and won three awards – it's unbelievable.'

They were easily beaten on the day by Boyzone, who collected six awards, but the measure of the differing impact of the two groups was clear when writer Simon Sebag-Montefiore from the *Spectator* was waiting backstage later to interview the girls, not the Dublin group. The *Spectator* is a heavyweight right-wing political magazine and just about the most unlikely publication to want an interview with a teen pop group. The idea had come from its editor who thought it would be fun, in view of the forthcoming general election, to interview the hottest pop star of the moment from a political perspective for the magazine's Christmas-New Year edition. The editor later revealed he wasn't even sure who the Spice Girls were when he had the idea, but, by the time the article was published, he was in no doubt, nor were millions of the older generation in Britain.

Before the celebrated *Spectator* article was published, the Spice Girls caused chaos in London's West End when they turned on the Oxford Street Christmas lights in front of 5,000 fans. Traffic was held up, fans of all ages screamed for the girls, but it was a tiny commotion compared to the media blitz the following week.

'Maggie was the first Spice Girl' was the sound bite which captured the headlines from the *Daily Star* to the *Financial Times*. During the *Spectator* interview the girls had spoken on many political subjects, their love of Margaret Thatcher's ideals, fears for Britain joining the single currency with Europe and their suspicions about Labour leader Tony Blair's ability to be Prime Minister. Yet the newspapers seized on the Thatcher angle, principally because it came when the Tory government was being ripped to shreds in all quarters.

Predictably, it was Geri who had come out with the headline-grabbing gem. She had said, 'We Spice Girls are true Thatcherites.

Thatcher was the first Spice Girl, the pioneer of our ideology, Girl Power. Thatcher had ideals all right – we love Maggie.' She also added, 'We met Tony Blair and he seemed nice enough. His hair's all right, but we don't agree with his tax policies. He's just not a safe pair of hands for the economy.' Victoria went on to say they would never vote Labour, but also added that John Major was a 'boring pillock'.

The publicity brought page after page of coverage and political analysis. Did this reflect the views of the youth generation, columnists wondered? The girls were even being talked about in the corridors of the House of Commons. Baroness Thatcher's office said she would be 'thrilled' by the girls' comments, while the Tory Central Office issued a statement which read, 'They obviously have very clear political views. They are a go-ahead group and we are a go-ahead party.' At least the Labour Party maintained a sense of humour and said, 'Just because the Spice Girls like Margaret Thatcher, it won't stop Tony Blair liking their music.'

Simon Sebag-Montefiore said of his article, 'It was light hearted, but there is a serious side. The Spice Girls are influencing a whole generation of youngsters and no one really knows how that generation thinks. It was a very pleasant interview. These are no bimbos. I expected them to espouse typical left-wing pop star politics, with a few pathetic ideas on the legalisation of heroin and some fuzzy thoughts on individuality and community policies, but I found them bright, articulate and with a full grip of the great issues of the day.'

The writer may have been happy, but the girls were certainly not when they saw the headlines, some illustrated with pictures of them superimposed outside 10 Downing Street. They were all angry to be labelled Thatcherites, particularly Mel B because she's an anarchist and Mel C because she's a Labour supporter. She later told the *Face*, 'We are all very young girls and half of us haven't got a clue about politics for a start. I don't vote any more because I don't know enough about politics to vote. I think you should be taught in school about politics. When I voted, I voted Labour. I'm from working-class Liverpool. Can you imagine the stick I got when all that was in the paper? My dad really frightened me. He said, "Margaret Thatcher? You want to watch yourself when you go back to Liverpool." I think Margaret Thatcher is a complete p**** after what she's done to my hometown.' Even Geri was angry because she had been praising Thatcher for becoming the first woman Prime Minister, not for all her policies.

However, after all the ridiculous hype and analysis resulting from that interview, the best comment came from Emma. She probably gave a clearer guide to what most of the young generation thinks – or, rather, doesn't think – about politics when she said, 'We had the big interview and I didn't say anything. I didn't even talk and there was a picture of me outside 10 Downing Street. I don't think I'll vote – am I allowed to say that? Do I think Margaret Thatcher was the original Spice Girl? Not particularly. My mum is.'

As the political fallout settled, Spice Girls mania continued to spread. It was reported that one of the most popular new pastimes among men was discussing who was their favourite Spice Girl – but it was a subject responsible for causing countless rows with girlfriends and wives. Emma got the Royal seal of approval when it was revealed that fourteen-year-old Prince William had replaced his poster of *Baywatch* star Pamela Anderson with one of her in his bedroom at Eton.

The planned release of the third single, '2 Become 1', clashed with the children of Dunblane's tribute song, 'Knockin' on Heaven's Door', so it was delayed. Once it was released, the Spice Girls chalked up their third No .1, following sales of 209,000 copies in the first three days alone. 'Say You'll Be There' was still at No. 17 in the charts and Madonna, the original queen of the Wannabees, had to settle for No. 3 with her new release, 'Don't Cry For Me Argentina' from the film *Evita*.

On Sunday, 22 December, the Spice Girls were confirmed as the Christmas No.1. It was time for more celebrations, unless, that is, you were a bookmaker. Despite closing the betting on the Christmas chart early, they still had to pay out £92,000 – their worst loss for years.

In six breathtaking months, the Spice Girls had gone from nowhere to have three consecutive No. 1 UK hits, a No. 1 album and No. 1s in two dozen countries. Their three singles had all gone platinum with sales exceeding 600,000 each and the album had sold 1.8 million. As Mel C reflected on their achievements she said, 'Mad! Totally messed-up and mad. This has been the craziest, most knackering year of our lives!'

Things had got so mad that someone even crept up to Geri's flat and stole her rubbish!

– 10 –

HITTING THE
JACKPOT

As the Spice Girls, their manager, and the executives at Virgin looked forward to building on the success of the previous six months, nothing could have prepared them for what lay in store in 1997. The girls' popularity had proved so widespread that their schedule was already jam-packed for the next eighteen months with an amazing itinerary which would take them around the world as well as headline some of the most important pop music events. The principal aim for the early part of the year was to break into the notoriously difficult American market, but before they embarked on any work, the girls were allowed a well-earned holiday to re-energise their Girl Power for the gruelling year ahead.

Most of the girls headed to islands in the Caribbean. Geri went to Antigua and Mel B visited her grandmother and other relatives on Nevis. Emma paid for her family and boyfriend, Mark, to stay at a luxury resort in Barbados, but the holiday was ruined when a photographer staked out the hotel and took photos of her in a swimsuit. Emma was reduced to tears when the pictures were published back home with bitchy comments that she had 'chunky hips and thighs'.

The photos were the first in a series of personal upsets which would hit the girls once they came back from holiday to start work. Their personal lives would become deeply affected by stardom and among the first casualties were boyfriends. Geri wasn't in a serious relationship, but she had been going out with Giovanni Laporta, a double-glazing businessman she had known for a while and bumped into at a Christmas party. He revealed she'd not had sex for two years before dating him, but that didn't stop her dumping him in true Girl Power fashion after just a few weeks. As she packed her bags for the Spice Girls' trip to Canada and North America in late January, she decided to pack Giovanni in, too, by leaving a typed note at his house. Giovanni told one newspaper, 'She finished with me and I'm not happy. She didn't even have the decency to tell me to my face. I thought she might call me and tell me I'm dumped but she didn't say anything. I knew it wasn't going anywhere, she knew it wasn't going anywhere. There was too much pressure, but I don't care about Geri. I only started dating her because it was a challenge. She was a Spice Girl, after all.'

The only challenge Geri was interested in now was making the Spice Girls as successful as possible. One giant leap was taken towards that goal during the promotional tour of Canada and North America. 'Wannabe' entered the US Billboard Top 100 chart at No. 11, tying with Alanis Morisette for the highest entry for a début act. By the time the girls arrived in New York, some critics were already hailing them as the biggest pop import from Britain since the Fab Four. The media and the paparazzi were there in force to greet them, even people in the streets of the Big Apple were singing 'Wannabe' to the girls as they ventured out of their hotel to do various interviews. After a week of promotion, the single moved to No. 6 and the buzz started to reach Britain that they were heading for the top. The only blight on the triumphant trip to America was a poor live performance in front of 2,000 people at a fairground in Miami. They mimed to their backing track, which left the crowd unimpresssed. Mel B was criticised in the press for giving the crowd a V-sign as she left the stage, but she revealed later it was a Girl Power salute, not an insulting gesture. Following the disappointment of that gig, the Spice Girls kept their promotion work restricted to TV and radio shows.

Behind the scenes, the success in America had already helped seal a huge, ground-breaking sponsorship deal with Pepsi. Details of the link-up wouldn't be revealed for many months, but during that trip the girls jetted to Los Angeles to film a secret video for the forthcoming promotion. To have a huge market player such as Pepsi aboard was a clear sign of the girls' global appeal.

Soon after arriving back in London, the Spice Girls were celebrating 'Wannabe' reaching No. 1 in the States. On Thursday, 13 February, four weeks after its release, it finally knocked Toni Braxton's 'Un-break My Heart' off the top. The Spice Girls went into the record books again to be the first British group to have a US No. 1 with their début single. The Beatles only managed No. 12 with 'I Want To Hold Your Hand' in 1964. 'Wannabe' became the first British song to get to No. 1 there since Seal's 'Kiss From A Rose' two years earlier, and already the girls were eclipsing established groups such as Oasis, Blur and Take That, who had had seven hits in Britain but had only got to No. 7 in America with 'Back For Good'. America became the thirty-first country where 'Wannabe' hit No. 1 and while they celebrated the girls were given even more good news – *Spice* had gone to No. 6 in the US album charts.

Geri said, 'It's just amazing. I don't think any of us can believe what's gone on in the last year. We've gone from complete unknowns to having number ones all over the world. It's a bit hard to take it all in. Everyone has been amazed at how fast we've hit America, especially us. We've done it even faster than the Beatles. Now everyone is expecting us to up sticks and move over there for good, but we'd never do it – we love Britain too much and we're dead proud to be British. We owe all our success to Britain and we're proud to be ambassadors of pop for our country.'

The girls were given the news about 'Wannabe' while shooting the hilarious video for their next single, 'Who Do You Think You Are?' in West London with the Sugar Lumps, a spoof of the group, starring singer Lulu and the British comedy duo French and Saunders. The single would be released as a double A-Side with 'Mama' to raise money for the Comic Relief charity fund.

Hardly before the celebrations had ended, the Spice Girls were raising their glasses again after receiving five nominations for prestigous Brit Awards. A year earlier the girls had been taken to the glittering ceremony as awestruck new signings to Virgin, but now they were told they would be opening the 1997 show at London's Earls Court. Oasis singer Liam Gallagher caused a stir in the run-up to the event by refusing to attend because he would 'probably chin the Spice Girls'. It was the opening bell in a verbal bout between the two groups which would be slugged out for months.

The evening itself got off to a bizarre start when a cover group of Spice Girls lookalikes calling themselves A Touch Of Spice fooled fans and security guards when they arrived at the arena in a white limousine. They were mobbed, interviewed by TV crews, and led to the VIP dressing rooms before they were rumbled – because the real Spice Girls were already there!

An indication of how far the girls had come since their first visit to the Brits was the company they mixed with backstage. They were unashamed star spotters as they rubbed shoulders with some of the greats of music and had their photo taken with numerous stars, including Elton John, Diana Ross and Gary Barlow. Geri said, 'We had a brilliant time and were behaving like fans. We kept seeing all these famous people. When Diana Ross came up to us we just had to have our photo taken with her. She's a legend.' Emma added, 'Last year no one knew who we were and no one took our picture. We were walking around gobsmacked, just glad to be there. A year on, and we're opening the show – and people we don't even recognise know our names.'

Despite being among so many greats of the record industry, the Spice Girls stole the show and the next day's headlines with a raunchy and cheeky performance throughout the night. They opened the event in front of 1,000 VIPs with a storming – mimed – version of 'Who Do You Think You Are?' Their outfits brought cheers from the fans in the front of the stage and gasps from the dinner-suited guests sitting at tables beside the runway. In particular, Geri's Union Flag micro-dress, which finished above her underwear, was the talk of the night and the subject of countless fashion articles in the ensuing weeks.

The girls picked up awards for Best Single for 'Wannabe' and Best Video for 'Say You'll Be There', which were both chosen by public votes, as opposed to executives within the industry. As the girls accepted the Best Video award Mel C made a provocative challenge to Liam Gallagher, 'I would just like to say – Liam, come and have a go, if you think you're hard enough.' The comment brought further cheers from the audience, but, again, it was Geri's attire which was the focus of attention. She had changed for the awards collection into a figure-hugging scarlet sequined dress, which was so low-cut it couldn't contain her breasts. As they popped out twice in full view of the audience and TV cameras, she laughed, 'If you wear a tight dress like this, you've got to expect it. Everyone has seen them before, so I don't give a damn. This is the best night of our lives ever, so I don't care what happens.'

The girls certainly made the most of the night. Their manager Simon Fuller threw a private party at a fashionable restaurant in

Soho where they partied well into the early hours with a host of celebrities. Geri outlasted them all and even went on to another party when their bash finished around 4 am. She had to laugh the next morning when she woke up feeling jaded only to see herself plastered all over the newspapers glorified as a sex symbol. She said, 'It's hilarious that we're called sex symbols – I don't think I'm some goddamn sexy woman at all. I'm like any other woman in the world. When I get up in the morning I look in the mirror and I think, Oh no, where's my make-up bag? This morning, I staggered out of bed and sat next to my brother-in-law who was looking at a picture of me in the paper. He looked at me, looked at the picture again, then burst out laughing. I mean, how can I be a sex symbol? I'm clumsy, not sexy. I have the same insecurities most women have and I drag myself down the gym when I can to improve on what I've got. But I like that about all of us. We're proof that you don't have to be classically beautiful, or six feet tall, to be considered attractive. None of us has model looks and, hopefully, we are role models for young girls because of that. If anyone thinks I'm sexy, then that's really nice – but I can't see it myself.'

On 3 March, the double A-side 'Mama'/'Who Do You Think You Are?' was released with profits going to Comic Relief. The following Sunday – appropriately, Mothering Sunday – it went straight to No. 1 and gave the girls another place in the record books, making them the first group to reach the top with their first four singles. The previous record holders were jointly Gerry And The Pacemakers, Frankie Goes To Hollywood and Jive Bunny, who all had three. The Spice Girls now topped the charts on both sides of the Atlantic, a feat not reached since Tiffany in 1988 with 'I Think We're Alone Now'. Worldwide CD sales for the girls had now reached six million albums and seven million singles. 'Wannabe', then in its fourth week at No. 1 in the States, accounted for four million of those sales, making it the most successful début single ever. Estimates put the girls' royalties and merchandising earnings at approaching £3 million each, although it would take many months before that money would flow through to them.

Amidst all the good news for the girls, there was also a positive break for the men who had started their dream. Bob and Chris Herbert announced plans to start a new boy band and had held auditions similar to the ones for the girls back in 1994. They had selected their line-up, which would be called Five, and had decided on a streetwise image similar to what they had wanted for the girls. The Herberts had gained so much kudos within the music business for starting the Spice Girls that Five landed a big contract within weeks of their formation, so maybe the Herberts will yet get to manage a hugely successful act.

Meanwhile, the girls they had discovered continued to soar and had become the most sought-after celebrity launch guests. Car giants Mercedes paid for them to perform at Alexandra Palace in North London in an extravagant ceremony to unveil the new McLaren Formula 1 racing car. The girls also launched the mid-week National Lottery draw and, at the end of March, they caused a sensation in Central London when they pressed the 'on' button for Britain's new terrestial TV station, Channel 5.

The Spice Girls had now even transcended political consciousness in the build up to the general election when Labour leader Tony Blair included 'Wannabe' in his top-ten Desert Island Discs – even though he could only name three of the girls when asked during a separate TV interview. Also, Chancellor Kenneth Clarke, the man in charge of Britain's economy, parodied the song's lyrics in a speech saying, 'All I want, all I really, really want is a strong economy with low inflation...' Social analysts were even claiming that the Spice Girls phenomenon reflected a change in mood in British society and marked the return of the feel-good factor following the dark years of recession.

Despite all the positive aspects to their fame, the girls themselves were experiencing some problems. It was revealed that Geri had been haunted by a sex pest who made more than thirty obscene phone calls to her home which had left her terrified. It was reported that Geri decided not to make an official complaint to the police after she discovered that she knew the caller.

The other girls were having difficulties with their boyfriends. The pressures of fame had driven a gulf between Emma and Mark, while Victoria and her new boyfriend Stuart Bilton were also having problems. Although the girls had never denied having boyfriends, they had been obliged to keep them in the background. It soon proved to be an impossible task to keep a normal relationship together while being pop superstars.

Mark, who had met Emma just weeks before she had joined the group, told the *Mirror* newspaper, 'I was the boyfriend who wasn't supposed to exist. I was Mr Invisible. I had to duck down if we were ever spotted in a car together. Like the other Spice Girls, Emma had to be seen to be single and available. She was almost in tears when she told me she had to hide me from the world. She said, "I love you with all my heart and I'm so proud of you, But I'm not meant to have a boyfriend. It is not good for my image. It's going to be hard work. Do you think you can cope?" I held her hand, looked into those big blue eyes and said, "I loved you before you were famous and I would do anything to keep you." But, by the end, it was tearing me apart. To be kept on the sidelines helpless while your girlfriend is being lusted after and chatted up by some of the country's most successful men is simply soul destroying.

'She still rang me from wherever she was in the world, but instead of being an hour long, her calls were only five minutes. On the few days she wasn't travelling, filming or recording, she rarely managed to see me. In the end, my pride couldn't take it any more. I felt as if seeing me was a duty for her. From seeing her every day, I saw her once a month. Even when Emma did see me, I felt it was rushed. She'd grown out of me, but she couldn't bring herself to accept it. She wasn't the girl I had fallen in love with. She was a Spice Girl now, adored by millions. There was no room for me in her life. Emma was the love of my life as well as my best friend. The Spice Girls may be the biggest group in the world, but I'm sorry she ever joined them.'

Emma felt the pain of the break up, too, but it was better to admit it was over than to go on living a lie. She was now living in a different stratosphere to Mark and it was too much to expect that a relationship that had begun before her fame could carry on under such a fierce spotlight.

Victoria had the same problems with Stuart and, even though they were planning to get engaged and buy a house together, they split up. Stuart said, 'I'd like to think we can still remain friends, but if she doesn't want to know, there's nothing I can do about it.' The difficulty of the break up must have been compounded when, only a short while later, it was revealed that Victoria was already enjoying a more glamorous love match with Manchester United's golden-boy footballer David Beckham. It emerged that they had met at a match earlier in March and had gone on a double date with Mel C and Ryan Giggs. Beckham seemed a perfect catch for Posh Spice, who admitted in one interview, 'Ambition turns me on – a man who knows what he wants and goes and gets it. I'm attracted to men with a lot of control and success, real go-getters. Success is always a turn-on.' How could Stuart Bilton, who worked in his mother's florists, compete with one of the world's most talented and good-looking footballers?

Mel B was the only other Spice Girl in a serious relationship. She had been with jewellery engraver Richard Meyer for two years. Their relationship continued for a few more months but then ended, and Mel began dating Icelandic businessman Fjolnir Thorgeirsson.

As the tears dried over their various love complications, the Spice Girls were free to enjoy the mad, exciting world of stardom with clear consciences. They headed to the Far East for promotional work, then checked into a luxury resort in Bali for a short break. But it seemed that wherever the Spice Girls appeared, controversy naturally followed. They only made two small public appearances at hotels while on the island, but at once they managed to create a minor international incident. For fun, some rugby players staying in one of the hotels taught the girls how to do the Ka Mate Haka – the traditional dance of the Maoris of New Zealand. The dance is made famous by the country's All Blacks rugby team. The Spice Girls caused hysterics at the hotel as they did the thigh-slapping, tongue-poking dance, but it put tribal leaders on the warpath because the dance is only meant to be done by men.

Maori leader Joe Harawira said, 'It's totally inappropriate for women to do this. It's not acceptable at all in our culture and to hear that it's been performed by girlie pop stars from another culture is unbelievable.' Rather more menacingly, Maori dance expert Willie Jackson added, 'The Spice Girls are on dangerous territory rubbishing our culture and worse still mocking our Haka. It's a bloody disgrace. We're sick of people bastardising our culture and we have a way of dealing with them.'

The Spice Girls were amazed their moment of fun had caused such outrage, but took the complaints seriously. Their spokesman said, 'It has never been their intention to upset anybody. They were only following the rugby players who didn't explain the significance of Ka Mate Haka. They absolutely didn't want to anger anyone. They regret upsetting anyone.'

If the reaction to the Spice Haka had been daft, it wasn't anything compared to some of the silliness surrounding the mania for the girls back in Britain. Van driver Joseph Marsden, from Coventry, was so besotted with Victoria he paid £100 to have an eight-inch tattoo of her pricked into his thigh. The girls had also inadvertently caused the break-up of at least one relationship. Jane Cleere dumped her boyfriend Sacha Hayward because he was obsessed with the group. He had posters on his walls and even played their music while they were making love. Finally, Jane snapped and walked out claiming, 'There wasn't room for seven of us in the relationship. Sacha was totally obsessed. I told him it was either them, or me, and he chose them. Everything was wonderful until those girls came along. Now I never want to hear them again.' Sacha hit back, 'I'm upset she dumped me, but I'm even more upset about my posters and broken CDs.'

Even schools were feeling the knock-on effects of Girl Power. Blonde schoolgirl Carly Austin dyed her hair red to be like Geri, only to be sent home by the head mistress in disgrace with orders to get her Baby Spice colour back. And the head teacher at a primary school in Derbyshire banned girls from practising their Spice Girls routines in the playground because it was too raunchy and was causing rivalry problems.

However, one group of fans were allowed to pretend to be their favourite Spice Girl, so they donned wigs, make up and wild outfits, and then went on national television to sing a hilarious version of 'Wannabe'. The only difference to this spoof group was that under the Spice Girls outfits were Boyzone!

Soon after arriving back from Bali, the girls finally received the only reward missing from their success – hard cash. They may have been selling millions of CDs and re-writing the record books, but the money was taking some time to flow through. Newspapers were speculating that the girls were already worth £5 million each, but a meeting with their accountant revealed their true worth to be a little more modest – well, for now, at least. Soon after the meeting, Mel C said, 'We were really disappointed because he said, "I'm sorry to tell you girls that the newspapers have been exaggerating slightly." We haven't got as much as we thought, just more that we'd got before.'

For girls who were on the dole less than two years earlier, it was certainly a bumper pay-out and they all enjoyed spending sprees. The first cheques went to help out their families in various ways. Mel C and Emma gave their mums the go-ahead to look for new homes, while Mel B cleared her parents' £25,000 mortgage. Victoria, Mel B and Geri splashed out on convertible sports cars. One of Victoria's first stops in her new car were the designer fashion stores of Knightsbridge for a massive spend.

The girls needn't have worried about blowing the entire amount from their pay-out because their popularity was soaring by the day. News came through that the album was climbing the American charts steadily, so they flew over to give their first totally live performance. For months now the sniping from critics had been getting louder because the Spice Girls had only ever mimed to backing tapes. It was the only dull mark on the sheen of their success, so they decided it was time to wipe it clean by singing on the *Saturday Night Live* programme, which has a regular audience of 20 million across the States. The girls sang 'Wannabe' and 'Say You'll Be There'and brought the studio audience screaming to their feet. Most of the American critics were also impressed and the *New*

York Daily News said, 'The Spice Girls certainly are singers and certainly are lookers. They had male hearts beating a bit faster across the nation.'

Emma admitted later, 'It was so scary, such a big challenge. We started off a little nervously, but then suddenly I think we all got into our stride. We have always been sure of our own talent, but now that we've proved it live we are more confident than ever. We all had a great buzz doing the show.'

News of the triumphant appearance on American TV marked an even greater escalation of interest in the Spice Girls. Media attention reached unbelievable proportions with Spice Girl exclusives and reports of their latest publicity stunts filling the pages of newspapers every day. Whatever they did made the headlines. One of the bigger announcements was the link-up with Pepsi. Dressed in specially designed Pepsi logo outfits, the girls unveiled the unique deal, which would include a special single, 'Step To Me', only available to Pepsi drinkers, and the corporation would also back the first full Spice Girls concert, to be staged in Istanbul, Turkey, in October 1997 for 40,000 fans. Turkey was chosen because it is where East meets West and was considered an appropriate venue for fans worldwide.

The fizz from the Pepsi announcement had no time to go flat before the Spice Girls were gearing up for, arguably, their most important performance to date: their first live gig in Britain. They rehearsed thoroughly for the Prince's Trust twenty-first anniversary concert at the Manchester Opera House, but their short performance was nowhere near as slick as their showstopper in America. The girls, however, made up for their lack of power on-stage by ambushing Prince Charles in the formal line-up after the concert. First Mel B planted a big kiss on his cheek and was swiftly followed by Geri. The Prince was left stunned and with two large red lipstick marks on his cheeks. It was a blatant breach of Royal protocol, and very risky even for the Spice Girls, but Prince Charles took it in good humour. They teased him with a series of cheeky comments. Geri, dressed in a tiny blue and white trapeze artist outfit, said, 'I think you're very sexy. We could spice up your life.' The girls also tried to get Charles to do the Girl Power V-sign, although he resisted. But the biggest show of cheek came from Geri when she pinched his bottom.

The Prince laughed off the ambush in his speech to the audience a few moments later, but even then Geri was seen in the background flicking her head back to get in the TV camera shot. Her behaviour was considered several steps beyond the mark by some people, but she shrugged it off. She said later, 'We didn't plan to ambush him – it just happened. We treat everyone the same, whether they're a prince or a postman. I pinch everyone's bottom, so why stop at Prince Charles? I'll pinch Tony Blair's if he ever walks past me!'

With barely time to touch up their lipstick, the Spice Girls were off on the next adventure – the Cannes Film festival. Cannes has played host to just about every big celebrity ever over the years, but the girls had no problem staking their claim in the town's hall of fame. They arrived wearing headscarves and sunglasses in the style of screen goddesses of the 1940s, then proceeded to steal the show in true Hollywood style. They appeared on top of the Hotel Martinez entrance for their photocall and brought the area to a standstill. Hundreds of photographers and film crews from around the world jostled for position, while fans and passersby climbed on roofs and lampposts to get a look. It was one of the most chaotic photocalls ever seen at the festival – and this was for five girls who hadn't even made a movie.

The frenetic media scenes continued at a press conference where the girls revealed details of their forthcoming film, *Spice – The Movie*, a comedy in the mould of the Beatles' *A Hard Day's Night*. The film would be set in London and follow five mad days in the girls' lives, with actor Richard E. Grant starring as their neurotic manager and a host of other celebrities in cameo roles. The girls showed they didn't need a script to be funny when they turned the press conference – traditionally dreary affairs – into hilarious fun. Even cynical showbiz hacks, so used to Hollywood egomaniacs giving monosyllabic answers, were won over by the girls' witty comments and general unaffected sense of fun. The girls spared no one. They teased and poked fun at the journalists as they nervously asked questions. One was told off for crossing his arms because it was 'bad body language', another was ribbed for his thinning hair, and one poor nervous writer was ridiculed for stammering through his question. One correspondent from Lebanon wistfully asked, 'Are you coming to visit us?' and Mel C quipped, 'Oh, we've never been to Lebanon, but I've been to Debenhams lots of times!'

When the atmosphere became too serious, Geri insisted the journalists do a Mexican wave, or they wouldn't answer any more questions. Amazingly, the press obliged. One British showbiz journalist who was there said, 'It really was hilarious. Most of those press conferences are a bore and a sham. The stars pose for a while and grudgingly answer a few stupid questions then go. But the Spice Girls were in a different class. They didn't give a damn about posing and were determined to have a laugh. They made a show of it and won a lot of people over.' The girls led the press on another merry dance on boats as they made their way to a private beach for an exclusive French TV appearance. They then settled on a £8 million yacht for more interviews before partying the night away at Planet Hollywood with supermodels Naomi Campbell and Kate Moss and other celebrities.

Fresh after their Cannes triumph, the Spice Girls flew to New York to celebrate one of the best pieces of news to date – after two months in the charts, the album *Spice* had gone to No. 1 in America, making them the first British group to top the US charts with a début album. The Beatles' first album, *Introducing The Beatles*, was held off the top spot by their second, *Meet The Beatles*. To add to the excitement 'Say You'll Be There' went into the US charts at No. 5 on the same day. The girls sang the single on David Letterman's *The Late Show* and then toasted their success in Manhattan. Mel B said, 'We can't believe the album is top of the chart – it's mind-blowing. We were hoping to get in the top ten, but not this.' Geri added, 'It's great. This isn't luck – we have worked damned hard for it.' And in a joint statement the girls declared, 'Pop is back by Girl Power demand and we're thrilled. This proves that with hard work and determination you can do anything. The encouragement of our fans has helped us in our mission to conquer America.'

Three weeks later, the album was still at No.1, but the girls were already celebrating a new achievement. They were honoured in London with two prestigious Ivor Novello songwriting awards – Best British Single and Best International Hit for 'Wannabe'. The awards ceremony was on Mel B's twenty-second birthday and, in an attempt to orchestrate the audience as she had done in Cannes, Geri tried to get the VIPs to sing Happy Birthday. This time, however, they weren't in such an obliging mood.

One moment probably sums up the Spice Girls more than any high profile media event they shine at these days. It came one Friday afternoon in June as Shelley D'Silva, the girl who helped discover the Spice Girls, was being driven along the Embankment in London heading out of town. It was a fine day, so her boss's smart Saab convertible had its roof down. Suddenly, a shiny black Range Rover, its windows tinted black, pulled up beside them. Leaning out of one of the back windows was Geri, screaming and waving excitedly. 'Shelley! Shelley!' Shelley looked up in shock and Geri asked 'How are you?' She just had time to answer and return the question before the Rover gunned ahead. Geri was smiling widely and yelling, 'We're fine ... we're fine', and then the car turned off. Just before it was out of sight, Shelley could see some other familiar faces squeezing out the window, their hands waving.

It sums up the life of the Spice Girls: everything done at a breathless pace, always racing forward at full throttle, but, thankfully, with one eye still on where they've come from, even if it is becoming more blurred by the minute. Shelley was touched by the gesture that day. They could so easily have driven passed; many celebrities would ignore someone from their more humble days. But Shelley had been instrumental in putting the girls on the road to fame and, clearly, Geri remembers things like that and, hopefully, so do all the girls. As long as they retain that knowledge, remember those days in the dented Fiat, and keep their sense of humour – especially amidst all the pretence of showbusiness – then everyone will want the comfortable limo ride to continue for many, many miles yet.

~

In less than a year since the release of 'Wannabe', the Spice Girls had reached heights beyond their wildest dreams. They had chalked up No.1 hits in thirty-one countries and surpassed chart records set by the Beatles. They had sold 14 million singles and 10 million copies of *Spice* which was still in the top three in the British charts seven months after its release, and still at No. 1 in the US charts after four weeks – stopping the ex-Beatle himself, Sir Paul McCartney, from reaching the top there with his album *Flaming Pie*.

The Spice Girls machine seems unstoppable. They have already applied for trademarks in more than a hundred categories which will see a deluge of Spice Girls merchandise, from toothpicks and perfume, to computer software and hi-fi equipment, to possibly even cars carrying their individual nicknames. With the movie, a new album, which will undoubtedly spawn many more No. 1 singles, the Turkey concert, and a world tour due to begin in February 1998, the Spice Girls party is still in full swing. As Geri puts it, 'The Spice Girls will end when we stop having fun. Right now we are having *lots* of fun.'

The girls have come a long way since those exhausting, often tearful singing lessons with Pepi Lemer when they were hungry wannabees. Their bodies had ached from dancing and their voices were sore from repeating notes hour after hour. Pepi had looked into their ambitious eyes and warned, 'It's like a lottery, girls. Only one in a hundred million makes it.'

Well, the hand of fate did point its magic finger at Geri, Mel B, Victoria, Mel C and Emma. They have indeed scooped the pop music lottery – and the jackpot is still rolling over.

ABOUT THE AUTHOR

Rob McGibbon began his journalistic career on the *Wimbledon News* in South London, and worked as a news reporter and show-business writer on several national newspapers before leaving to write books.

In 1990 he co-wrote the first biography of the New Kids On The Block with his father, Robin, also a journalist. They gambled on publishing the book themselves, before the band were famous in Britain, and it became a worldwide bestseller. In the next three years, they wrote biographies of England footballer Paul Gascoigne, TV presenter Phillip Schofield and Simply Red's lead singer Mick Hucknall.

In addition, Rob has written a biography of Take That, a bestseller in Germany, and three other books for Boxtree – *Boyzone On The Road*, *The Official Backstreet Boys Story* and *Boyzone, The True Story*.

In between writing books, Rob is a freelance journalist writing mainly celebrity interviews. He lives in Chelsea, London. Among his many interests is soccer and, as a life-long Chelsea fan, one of his proudest sporting moments – apart from watching Chelsea win the 1997 FA Cup – was playing in a celebrity match at Stamford Bridge.